VIJÑAPTIMĀTRATĀSIDDHI

(VIṂŚATIKĀ)

VIJÑAPTIMĀTRATĀSIDDHI

(VIṂŚATIKĀ)

(With Introduction, Translation and Commentary)

T.R. SHARMA
M.A., Ph. D.

Eastern Book Linkers
DELHI : : (INDIA)

Publishers :
EASTERN BOOK LINKERS

H. O. : 5825, New Chandrawal,
Jawahar Nagar, Delhi-110007
Ph. : 23850287, 9811232913

Show Room : 4806/24, Bharat Ram Road,
Daryaganj, New Delhi-110002
Ph. : 23285413

e-mail : eblindology@gmail.com
eblinfo76@gmail.com
Website : www.eblindology.com

Edition : 2017

Rs. : ₹ 450

ISBN : 978-81-7854-341-3

VIJÑAPTIMĀTRATĀSIDDHI

By **T.R. Sharma**

Printed at : **R.K. Print Service, Delhi**

समर्पण

प्यारी बेटी सुपर्णा को
जो भविष्य की आनन्दमयी लहर को
असमय में छिन्न-भिन्न कर न जाने
कहाँ विलीन हो गयी !

PREFACE

It is indeed a very difficult task to talk with any amount of certainity of the commencement of *Vijñānavāda* because the genesis of the system may be traced book to the earliest stages of development of the Buddhist philosophy. It is only with regard to the standardised stage of any particular system of philosophy that we become fully aware of it as a full-fledged system of philosophy. From all records available to us, both historical and philosophical we may say that *Maitreya* may be regarded as a progenitor of the *Yogācāra / Vijñānavāda* school of philosophy.

According to the Tibetan tradition *Maitreya* is supposed to have written the five works viz., (i) *Sūtrālaṅkāra* (ii) *Madhyānta-Vibhaṅga,* (iii) *Dharma-dharmatā-vibhaṅga,* (iv) *Abhisamayālaṅkāra,* and (v) *Uttaratantra,* whereas the Chinese tradition enumerates the *Yogācārabhūmi, Yogavibhaṅga* (now lost), *Mahāyānasūtrālaṅkāra, Madhyāntavibhāga* and *Vajracchedikāvyākhyā* as the works of *Maitreya*. It must be obsreved that there are three different traditions of the nucleus of the philosophical ideas associated with the *Vijñānavāda,* viz, Chinese, Tibetan and Indian. As a result of modern researches it has been now possible that some of the works concerning idealism, which were earlier only available to us in Chinese and Tibetan traditions, have now been also transferred to Indian tradition. We may surmise that possibly there must have been some common stock of a rich philosophical ideas or concepts concerning idealism where from all the above said three different traditions might have derived their respective inspiration. According to some scholars the *Yogācārabhūmi* may be considered as a fundamental text of the *Yogācāra*.

The *Mahāyāna* school of Buddhist philosophy is represented by the *Mādhyamika* and *Vijñānavāda* and it may be said that the two are not fundamentally different from each other in the ultimate analysis. Hajime Nakamura says in this regard, "The philosophy of viodness presented before us with the following principal doctrines; Voidness, Dependent Origination; Existence under conditions *(prajñapti)* and the middle way. They were all incorporated into the system of

Vijñānavāda, which is quite accomodating to the structure of human existence, and uses such terms as *dharmas, vijñānas, ālaya-vijñāna, pariṇāma, bīja, vāsanā* etc. in order to prove to educe the real fact of experience."[1] In Hīnayāna, the two earlier schools of philosophy viz., *Sautrāntikas* and the *Vaibhāṣikas* had accepted the external reality of the object (*artha*) whereas in the Mahāyāna, both the *Mādhyamika* and *Vijñānavāda*, denied the external reality of the object and both of them reduced the object to *śūnya* (void) and *vijñapti* (consciousness) respectively. Both schools had rejected the object at the phenomenal level (though accepting its physical existence) and had accepted it at the noumenal level. While doing so the *Vijñānavāda* schools of philosophy built a system which is called the doctrine of *Vijñaptimātra* or *cittamātra*.

In the *Yogācāra* philosophical system terms like *ālaya vijñāna, cittamātra, vijñāna* and *vijñaptimātra* are frequently used. They represent the central concepts in the works such as the *Sandhinirmocanasūtra* and *Laṅkāvatārasūtra*. Among all these terms *cittamātra* is undoubtedly one of the most complex and difficult term for a number of reasons. From its various usages both in the *Yogācāra* and *Mādhyamika* works it appears to be associated with (i) purely philosophical and the critical speculation and also (ii) with spiritual meditative pratices. It was also used to emphasize the primary importance of meditative technique as a means of gaining an unimpeded view of the ultimate reality. We should always be careful with regard to its changing context. The original concept of *vijñaptimātra* can be traced back to the *Sandhinirmocanasūtra*, from where Asaṅga quotes one passage in his *Mahāyāna-saṃgraha* :

'Maitreya asked : Lord, are these images cognised in meditation different from that mind (which cognises them) or are they not different ? The Lord answered; Maitreya, they are not different, And why ? Because those images are nothing but cenceptaulization (*vijñaptimātra*). Maitreya, I have explained that the meditative object (*alambana*) of consciousness (*vijñāna*) is comprised of (*prabhāvita*) nothing but conceptuliza-tion (*vijñāptimātra*).'

From the above quotation of Asaṅga it is quite clear that term like *cittamātra* and *vijñaptimātra* pertain to actual medita-

1. Indian Buddhism, Buddhist Tradition Series, ed. Alex Wayman, Delhi, 1989, pp. 254-255.

tive instruction and practice. Probably this may also appear to be one of the reasons for the system of philosophy of idealism to be called as *Yogācāra*. The *Yogācāra* is indeed concerned with mind (*citta*) its nature, development and its working.

It is well known that *Laṅkāvatārasūtra* is supposed to be the prominent work to have a full-blown idealism in it. Some scholars are of the view that this work is syncretic in nature. From its vast contents concerning idealism it can be said that it grew gradually collecting discussions on a great variety of topics which interested the idealistic movement. There is no doubt that this text has gone into the minutest possible detailed analysis of the mind (*citta*). It has established that the whole universe is just a manifestation of the mind (*citta*) itself. This very idea has found favour with most of the works dealing with *Yogācāra / Vijñānavāda* philosophy. However, we should note in passing that the *Laṅkāvatārasūtra* had identified the concept of *ālayavijñāna* with the concept of *tathāgatagarbha* and it may be pointed out that such an identification has not been acceptable by the early *Yogācāra* of Asaṅga Vasubandhu school.

Thus we see that the two works viz., *Sandhinirmocana-sūtra* and *Laṅkāvatārasūtra* provide us the basic infra - structure of the *Yogācāra* idialism.

The *vijñaptimātratā* or *cittamātrata* doctrine is contained in the twin works of *Viṃśatika* and *Triṃśika* of Vasubandhu, collectively named as *Vijñapatimātratāsiddhi*. According to some scholars the *Viṃśatikā* presents to us an analysis and description of the cause of ordinary beings' suffering while the *Triṃśikā* offers an analysis and description of the solutions to this problem.

The *Viṃśatikā* was first translated from Tibetan version into French by de la Vallee Poussin, Paris, 1912. The Sanskrit text was found and edited by S. Levi, Paris in 1925. It was also translated into French by S.Levi in 1932. Once the text of *Viṃśatikā* was found and edited, many other expositions by way of comparative study of Tibetan, Chinese, Japanese were undertaken by the Japanese and Chinese scholars. The great Chinese Buddhist scholar Hsüang-tsang (599-664) composed a Chinese version known as *Vijñaptimātratātridaśa-śāstrakārikā* (Wei-shih-san - shih-lun-sung). As for as its English translation is concerned; S.Bagachi translated it first into English in 1957, published under the series of Nalanda

Publication No.1. Thomas A. Kochumuttom has translated it into English under the title, 'A Buddhist Doctrine of Experience, Delhi, 1982. Another scholar Stefan Anacker has translated the *Viṃśatikā* under the title 'Seven works of Vasubandhu' Delhi, 1984. Anacker simply gives the English translation of the text followed by running footnotes. There is no doubt that these English renderings with notes have their own utility for students and scholars. But there are many contexts in it which require greater exposition giving the allied concepts or ideas from works of Buddhist philosophy.

It was in the academic year of 1988-89 that I was asked by the Department of Buddhist Studies, University of Delhi, to teach the *Vijñaptimātratāsiddhi (Viṃśatikā)*. English being the medium of instruction, I consulted some of the available English expositions. I must admit that all the above mentioned English renderings were very useful for my own understanding at the initial stage and specially Thomas A. Kochumuttom's 'A Buddhist Doctrine of Experience.' During the course of my study I consulted some of the Hindi expositions of *Viṃśatīka* and I found that this *Vijñaptimātratāsiddhi*, edited by Prof. Ram Shankar Tripathi., Varanasi, 1992 was helpful in understanding some of the difficult passages given therein. As far as my own understanding of *Yogācāra / Vijñānavāda* is concerned, I believe that A.K. Chatterjee's 'Yogācāra Idealism' greatly helped me in properly formulating some of my ideas concerning idealism. In preparing the present edition I have been greatly benefited by his book and I have extensively quoted him wherever necessary. In preparing some of the notes I have taken great help from Prof. Ram Shankar's Tripathi's *Vijñaptimātratāsiddhi*.

The whole of the book has been divided into two parts. The first part deals with the detailed introduction to *Vijñānavāda* giving the various facets of idealism including the important question; why *Vijñānavāda* is called *Yogācāra* ? A special sub-title, 'Perceptual Image and the Conceptual Image' has been added in the introduction highlighting the approach towards an object (*artha*) of the *Sautrāntikas* vs. *Vijñānavādins*. In the introduction is also discussed the refutation of atomism from various point of views including the points raised against atomism by Śaṅkara in his *Brahmasūtrabhāṣya*. At the end is given a detailed analysis of the text in which an attempt has been made to explain why the suffix '*tā*' has been added to *Vijñaptimātra*.

The second part deals with the translation and exhaustive notes on the text. I must make my position clear with regard to its English translation. If correctly judged, it is really a very difficult job to translate any philosophical text into English because no rendering into a different language can be said to be a satisfactory one for numerous reasons. All I can say is that I have tried to put the original Sanskrit ideas into English in a running way without damaging the spirit of the text. No claim can be made on the exposition to be a technical philosophical rendering of the original text. Our effort has been to trace some of the concepts of *Yogācāra* idealism to other allied works of Buddhist philosophy. All such material has been provided in the foot notes. Vasubandhu's ideas concerning the waking and dreaming stage, the relative position of the infernal guards and the hell inhabitants with regard to the torment they (hell inhabitants) visualise, his refutation of atomism and his attempt to give the scriptual evidences in order to prove the consciousness (*vijñapti*) to be truly real - all these have been explained in the commentary with the help of suitable examples and diagrams. In the end an appendix has been added giving the 30 *kārikās* of *Triṃśikā*.

First of all it is my duty to thank the Department of Buddhist Studies, University of Delhi for providing me an opportunity to teach this text at the post-graduate level. As a matter of fact, this opportunity offered me a suitable occasion for seriously pondering upon some of the basic problems associated with *Vijñānavāda*. I am extremely indebted to Dr. H.S. Prasad, Department of Philosophy, University of Delhi, for going through the manuscript and suggesting a number of improvements in the introduction. Another friend of mine, Dr. S.C. Goswami was always readily available for discussing some of the problems of the text during the course of its preparation. I am highly obliged to both of them for giving me inspiration to complete the book at an early stage.

I thank Shri Shyam Lal Malhotra, the proprietor, Eastern Book Linkers for his keen interest in publishing the book. I heartily thank Mr. A.S. Mathur, of Compu Media for putting my own typed manuscript into the laser form.

15th August, 1993 T.R. SHARMA

CONTENTS

PART I

Introduction to Vijñānavāda

1. Vasubandhu, His Life and Works

Vasubandhu is one of the most prominent figures in the development of Buddhist philosophy in India. He was the younger brother of *Asaṅga,* and lived in the 4th century A.D. The Indian monk *Paramārtha* (499-569 A.D.) compiled a biography of *Vasubandhu* in which the biography of his brother *Asaṅga* also is included. It is said that in the beginning he was a *Sautrāntika,* and wrote works from the *Hinayāna* point of view. During the later part of his life he was converted to *Mahāyāna* by his brother and teacher *Asaṅga.*

Among his early works is the most famous *Abhidharmakośa* and a *bhāṣya* on it. Though it is written from the standpoint of the *Sarvastivāda* school, with the *Sautrāntika* polemics against it, it is nevertheless an authority for all schools of Buddhist philosophy. It has a famous commentary known as *Sphutārthavyākhyā* by *Vaśomitra.* Although *Vasubandhu* is supposed to have written as many as thirty two works., the following are important ones :

1. *Madhyānta-vibhāga-śāstra* with a *bhāṣya* on it
2. *Tri-Svabhāva-nirdeśa*
3. *Viṃśatikā,* with its *vṛtti*
4. *Triṃśikā*
5. *Karmasiddhiprakarṇa*
6. *Paramārthasaptati*

Besides these works, *Vasubandhu* has also written commentaries on some of the works like;

Mahāyāna-Sūtrālaṅkāra, Pratītyasamutpāda, Daśabhumikasūtra, Mahāyānasaṅgraha, Dharma-dharmtā-vibhaṅga, Akṣayamatinirdeśa, Gayāśīrṣa, Saṇmukhdhāriṇī, Caturdharmaka etc.

Towards the end of his life, he is said to have become a devotee of *Amitābha* and to have written a work entitled *Aparimitāyuṣasūtropadeśa,* in which he gave expression to his longing for *Sukhāvatī.*

2. Viṃśatikā (Kārikā and Vṛtti)

As far as *Yogācāra / vijñānvāda* philosophy is concerned;

Viṃśatikā forming a part of the *Vijñaptimātratāsiddhi* is the most important one because it brings out the basic tenets of *Vijñānavāda* in a very lucid manner. The present work is a study of this crucial text. The *Viṃśatikā* is a brief treatise written in twenty two couplets (*kārikā*) with an auto commentary known as *vṛtti* written by *Vasubandhu* himself. It is a thorough defence of *Vasubandhu's* idealist theory of knowledge against realist's correspondence theory of knowledge. While quoting C.H. Hamilton, Kochumuttom says, "*Viṃśatikā* is often interpreted as providing answers to realism and thus as showing that the universe as representation - only still is a serious and tenable conception".[1] Stefan Anacker in the same vein observes, "Perhaps no work of *Vasubandhu* has been more consistently misunderstood than the Twenty Verses. It has frequently been used as an authoritative source for opinions that are in fact not even there."[2]

The text of the *Viṃśatikā* consists of twenty two couplets (*kārikās*). All along these *kārikās* there is a running commentary by *Vasubandhu* himself known as *vṛtti*. It may be pointed out that as far the understanding of main text, i.e., *Viṃśatikā* is concerned; the importance of the commentary cannot be underestimated because this commentary unfolds many of the subtle points enumerated in these *kārikās* in a very lucid and simple *Sanskrit*. Moreover, the special features of the commentary is its peculiarity of presuming some of the points that could be raised by the opponents such as the *Sautrāntrikas* and the *Vaibhāṣikas*. Keeping these possible objections by the opponents in view the commentary tries to answer all these objections. In a way it can be said that the commentary enhances the beauty of details in a very academic style which is far from being very subtle and boring. After a careful study of this commentary, it can be easily said that in the absence of this commentary a complete comprehension of the text of the *Viṃśatikā* would have been an impossible task. The text does not start with the Ist *kārikā* but starts with a commentorial statement that *citta, manas, vijñāna* and *vijñāpti* are synonymous. It is also said that here the usage of this word

1. Kochumuttom, A Buddhist Doctrine of Experience, Delhi, 1982, P. 164. (cf. C.H. Hamilton, Wei Shih Er Shin Lin or The Treatise in Twenty Stanzas on Representation Only, (New Haven, American Oriental Society, 1938, p.6).
2. Stefan Anacker, Seven Works of Vasubandhu, Delhi, 1984, p.157.

citta (mind) is intended to include all the mental states. The first *kārikā* states that every thing in the world is in consciousness only (*vijñaptimātra*) as all the external objects in the world prove to be unreal because of their false appearances like the objects of hallucination etc. The second *kārikā* raises four possible objections to this notion of consciousness, i.e., (i) restriction of place; (ii) restriction of time, (iii) non-restriction of moment series and (iv) functional viability (*kṛtya kriyā*). In order to refute these objections,the examples of dreams, ghosts, hells and the internal guards are brought into discussion and *Vasubandhu* brilliantly answers all the points raised by the *Sautrāntikas* and *Vaibhāṣikas* in this connection. Thereafter, a discussion starts whether the beings seen by the hell-dwellers are a product of their own deeds or they are visible to them as a result of the consciousness. The seventh *kārikā* raises a question : how is it that the impression of a deed is imagined somewhere and its fruit is imagined somewhere else ? Further, another question is discussed in *kārikā* whether the bases of knowledge (*āyatanas*) are preached by the lord for humble people with a hidden meaning (*neyārtha*) (*kārikā* 8). The nineth *kārikā* brings into discussion the question of seed (*bija*). Hereafter *Vasubandhu* takes up the issues of non-substantiality of a *pudgala* (*pudgalanairātmya*) and a *dharma* (*dharmamairātmya*). The *kārikās* beginning from 11th to 17th are devoted to a very serious refutation of atomism.[3] The 18th *kārikā* aims at the question as to why the dreaming and waking stages are not similar. Afterwards a very pertinent question has been raised and answered both in the *kārikā* and *vṛtti*. The question is: how do we explain the process of death in terms of *Vijñanavāda* traditions ? The probable answer to this very important question, as suggested by *Vasubandhu* is this : due to particular consciousness of other beings there is produced a transformation in other beings stopping the life organs as such. By death is meant cutting off stream of existence.[4] It is quite likely that most of the modern readers and thinkers may not agree with this possible explanation of death as suggested by *Vasubandhu*. The text comes to an end

---

3. Cf. Stefan Anacker : "Its ingenious refutation of atomism could stop even a twentieth century particle physicist thinking." (Seven Works of Vasubandhu, p.157).
4. Cf. जीवितेन्द्रियविरोधिनी काचिद् विक्रियोत्पद्यते, या सभागसन्ततिविच्छेदाख्य मरणं भवतीति वेदितव्यम् ।

by declaring that the consciousness (*vijñapti*) is the only reality in this world and all the objects are mere representations of consciousness.

3. Background of Yogācāra

It may be pointed out that in Buddhist philosophy a lot of emphasis has been laid on subjectivity. This subjctivity was always linked with the concept of reality. Another important feature of the Buddhist philosophy is the realm of experience. As far as the historical development of the Buddhist philosophy is concerned, there are different phases of it, which can easily be discerned in this connection, viz., the realistic phase, the critical phase and the idealistic phase. Thus the earliest phase of the Buddhist philosophical thought starts with the *Sarvāstivāda*. This name is very significant on account of its meaning, according to which everything (*sarvam*) exists. By this what is really meant is that all the elements of existence (*dharmas*) are real. Also associated with the *dharma* is a concept of wholes (*pudgalas*) which in itself is unreal (*prajñaptisat*). The *Sarvāstivāda* school of thought accepted as many as 75 *dharmas*. These *dharmas* are treated as objectively real. This school is broadly covered under *Theravāda*. It may also be pointed out that *Theravāda* exerted little or no influence on the later development of Buddhism. *Theravāda* does not present any new system. Originally it prevailed in Ceylon, Burma and other parts of South Asia. After this school there emerged another school of thought known as *Sautrāntika*. This school must be understood as *Sarvāstivāda* itself because the former does not have much to contribute to the overall philosophical development of *Buddhism*. The *Sautrāntrika* school of thought accepted only 43 *dharmas* and rejected the rest as subjective. As far as the metaphysical position of this school is concerned; it may be said that this school maintains that everything is transient and perishing (*anitya*); everything is devoid of selfhood or substantiality (*anātma*); everything is discrete and unique (*svalakṣaṇa*). As far as reality is concerned; this school accepts the reality of the objects of the external world. This school accepts *pratyakṣa* as a true evidence of knowledge. This school has a historical importance because on account of its metaphysics it paved the way for the later *Mahāyānistic* developments in the history of Buddhism. According to A.K. Chatterjee, "The *Sautrāntrika* prepared the way of the *Mādhyamika* on the one hand and the *Yogācāra* on the other, and is, in a sense, the parting of ways".[5]

It has been already said above that the whole of the Buddhist philosophical thought can be divided into three phases, viz., realistic, critical and idealistic. When the *Sautrāntika* school had rejected the reality of the *pudgala*, but had maintained that of the *dharma*, even this position was broadly challenged by the *Mādhyamika* dialecties in a very subtle manner. They revolutionized the whole of the thinking of earlier schools and rejected all the *dharmas* saying that they were unreal in themselves. Not only they rejected all the *dharmas* as unreal; but they tried to test every *dharma* by means of the law of the dependent origination (*pratītyasamutpāda*). The *Mādhyamika* school of thought declared that relativity is the hall-mark of all the *dharmas* : this very *dharma* being relative, lacks in reality. This in itself gave birth to what is generally known as critical analysis of the thing of the external world. The *Mādhyamika* system offered an analytical power by which every object could be reduced to a mere concept. What we do in this system is nothing but to put labels on various objects of the world according to our convenience. This convenience is broadly challenged by the *Mādhyamika* philosophy in a very subtle manner. The main functions of the *Mādhayamika* is to know the Reality. However, when we go deeper, what we find is that all the approaches to know the reality are view-points only. The *Mādhyamika* declares that on analysing these different approaches what is left is *śūnyatā*. This system of philosophy emphasised that every category of thought is infected with relativity and is therefore void of reality (*niḥsvabhāva*) and as such it is purely imaginary, subjective. According to this school, subjectivity is another name of relativity. Relativity is the mark of unreal, of the subjective. The *Mādhyamika* concludes that our entire experience is purely subjective; things have only an apparent existence (*saṃvṛtti*), in reality they are imaginary (*kalpita*) and subjective.

4. Sautrāntika Approach towards an Object

Thus we have seen above that the *Mādhyamika* philosophy rejected all the elements of existence (*dharma*) but

5. *The Yogācāra Idealism*, Delhi, 1975, pp. 6-7.

this extreme position could not be maintained for a long time. Indirectly, we may say that the position really paved the way for the emergence of the *Yagācāra/Vijñānvāda* school of thought in the domain of Buddhist philosophy. A.K. Chatterjee observes in this connection, "The denial by the *Mādhyamika* of all metaphysics seemed to be an unqualified nihilism and a barren skepticism, and we have the 'Third Swinging of the wheel', represented by the *yogācāra idealism*".[6] This was nothing but the beginning of the idealistic phase in the Buddhist philosophical thought. Thus the *Yogācāra* is the culmination of Buddhism. We have seen above that the *Sautrāntika* had laid much emphasis on the perception of object. Perception according to this school is the cognition of the ultimately real *dharmas*; but these *dharmas* are not static. They are undergoing incessant change. No *dharma* can stay for any duration of time. It is absolutely momentary (*kṣaṇika*). Now there arises a very serious problem on account of every object being momentary in nature. When the object is momentary, the cognition is also like that. But if the object and its cognition are both momentary, perception becomes an inexplicable riddle. Perception is a natural process in which mind comes into contact with the object through the sense organs and the result is the perceptual knowledge. This process takes numerous moments. When the object comes into contact with the mind in first moment, this is the first stage. This gives place to the second moment. When the second moment arrives, the first moment, when the mind got the cognition of the objects, is no longer there. This process goes on endlessly. One moment cannot possibly know another moment. Every successive moment is unaware of the previous moments and the actual moment of the perception is left behind. Thus when the following moment emerges, the object is left far behind much less the knowledge of it. So it is a very difficult situation in which nothing is known. This is a very peculiar position in which the earliest Buddhism was confronted in the beginning. This is known as the momentariness of things. We have just seen that the theory of the momentariness presented a number of difficulties for the *Sautrāntika* to be solved in a consistent manner. It is not that *Sarvāstivāda* and the *Sautrāntika* were not aware of these difficulties. There cannot be any reconciliation between a vast

6. Ibid. p.11.

flow of moments where every one is giving birth to the next moment. This presents a peculiar difficulty for a theory of knowledge of an object in relation to its cognition or perception. If the two moments are simultaneous, one cannot be supposed to determine the other. In this way we can see how the *Yogācāra* developed in these extreme conditions. But here it must also be clarified as to what the chronological order of all these philosophical systems is. *Yogācāra* made an attempt to solve these inconsistencies of the *Sautrāntika* positions. The *Mādhyamika* also made a similar effort though in a different fashion. Thus the *Sautrāntika* occupies a central position in the historical development of Buddhism. The basic question is : whether the emergence of the *Yogācāra* would have been possible without the intervention of *Mādhyamika* ? Another important question in this connection is : is the *Yogācāra* school the last phase ? A possible answer to this question has been offered by A.K. Chatterjee in the following words, "The *Mādhyamika* is a very extreme position. The *Sautrāntika* and the *Yogācāra* are both speculative system and are spiritually akin; the *Mādhyamika* is the champion of pure criticism entailing the rejection of all metaphysics. It appears to be an accidental episode between two speculative philosophies. Is it really so, or is the *Mādhyamika* a necessary step in the logical development of idealism ? The *Yogācāra* is therefore the natural sequence to *Sautrāntika* logic : the interrelation of the *Mādhyamika* is an accident which could have been dispensed with. The *Sautrāntika* prepared the ground for the emergence of the idealism also in another important respect. All these considerations tend to prove that the transition from the critical realism of the *Sautrāntika* to the *Yogācāra* idealism is a logical and a natural one, and that it does not stand in any necessity of being mediated by the *Mādhyamika* criticism".[7]

We have seen above that the *Sautrāntika* and the *Mādhyamika* schools of philosophy had been very active as far as the realistic and critical phase of philosophical reasoning was concerned. The *Sautrāntika* school had its own difficulty when it advocated the theory of momentariness whereas the *Mādhyamika* had taken very extreme position in declaring that everything is unreal and empty (*śūnya*). These two phases of realistic and critical reasoning really paved the way for the

7. Ibid. pp. 19-20.

emergence of the *Yogācāra / Vijñānavāda*. The given object, when considered from the above mentioned two positions, was very difficult to be a subject of knowledge in any way. In both these positions the object was merely unreal and the unreality of the objects led to reality of the consciousness of *Yogācāra/Vijnānvāda*.

5. Philosophical schools of Buddhism

The Buddhist historians maintain that there were eighteen philosophical schools of Buddhism, though there is a discrepancy with regard to the individual names and classification. The historical records show that after about a hundred years of Buddha's *nirvāṇa* there was a Buddhist congregation where the first division took place at the council of Vaishali. In this council 10,000 Vajjian monks were excommunicated by the *Sthaviras* (elders) on the pretext of interpretation of the ten rules of discipline. These Vajjian monks formed themselves into a greater order named *Mahāsāṅghikas*. The scholars believe that the origin of the *Mahāyāna* can be traced to this division. From this group of elders (*Mahāsāṅghikas*) appeared two different schools separately i.e., *Sarvāstivādins* and the *Sammitīyas*. It may be mentioned that all the eighteen schools claimed to be the followers of the master and embody the teachings of the Lord. Of all the eighteen schools the four schools i.e., *Sthaviravāda*, *Sarvāstivāda*, *Mahāsāṅghikas* and the *Sammitīyas* are the main schools whereas the others are not so prominent.

(i) Sthaviravāda : this was very prominent in the beginning, but gradually lost its influence from the time of Ashoka's regin (3rd Century). Finally it disappeared from its mainland; however it is still prevalent in Geylon, Burma and Thailand.

(ii) Sarvāstivāda (Vaibhāṣika) : this school can be said to be very close to the *Theravāda*. This derives its name from the fact that it accepts the existence of all the three times, present, fast and future. *Sarvāstivāda* is usually called the *Vaibhāṣika* also because it is a system based on the *Vibhāṣā*.[8]

This was a major school in the beginning and it exerted much influence on the latter Buddhism in general. It was widely accepted in the whole of the country but was most

---

8. *Abhdharmakośabhāṣya*, edited D.D.Shastri., Varnasi, 1987, p.15.
विभाषया दीव्यन्ति चरन्ति वा वैभाषिकाः विभाषां वा वदन्तिं वैभाषिकाः ।

influential in Kashmir and Gandhara. It had its extensive *Abhidharma* literature in Sanskrit but lost and during the reign of Kasnishka (125 A.D.) two commentaries known as *Vibhāṣā* and *Mahāvibhāṣā* were written to explain the view points of this school. According to Takakusa the *Mahāvibhāṣa* belongs to Kashmira and the *Vibhāṣā* belongs to Gandhara. The *Abhidharmakośa* of Vasubandhu is a major treatise of this school besides some of the other works like *Abhidharmahṛdaya* of Dharmottara.

The *Vaibhāṣika* school believes in the denial of substance and accepts the discrete momentary *dharmas*. This school perceived a self cause (*svabhāva*) in the cause and emphasized the identity of cause and effect. This conception of the self-cause (*svabhāva*) was extened to all phenomena including the human personality. The followers of school believed that the self-cause (*svabhāva*) of *dharmas* remain during all the three periods of time, present, past and future. *Dharma* is a generic term in Buddhist philosophy used in the sense of the ultimate factor or elements of existence. This school recognized 75 *dharmas* in all - 72 being the conditioned *dharmas* (*sanskṛta*) and 3 unconditioned *dharmas* (*asaṃskṛta*). These elements of existence are impermanent (*anitya*) momentary (*kṣaṇika*) and durationless. All these *dharmas* have been classified into aggregates (*skandhas*) bases of knowledge (*āyatanas*) and *dhātu*. According to this classification the individuals can be analysed into a number of states without any soul or substance. The aggretates (*skandhas*) are five: (i) form (*rūpa*) : (ii) feeling (*vedanā* : (iii) name (*saṁjñā*) : (iv) impression (*saṃskāra*) and (v) consciousness (*vijñāna*). The bases of knowledge (*āyatanas*) are twelve-six sense organs with corresponding six sense data. The *dhātu* is a further elaboration of the bases of knowledge (*āyatanas*).

(iii) **Sammatīyas** (also known as *Vātsīputrīyas*) : it is very unfortunate that no work belonging to this school has been available to us as yet, though some of its thought concerning the soul or self (*pudgala*) have been severally criticized by Vasubandhu in *pudgala-nairātyma*.[9] Generally condemned by other schools as heretics, the followers of this school believe in the doctrine of the individual (*pudgala-ātman*), a quasi-permanent entity, neither completely identical with nor different from mental states.

---

9. Cf. *Pudgalanairātmya* and *Dharmanairātmya*, infra pp.24-27.

(iv) Mahāsānghikas : this school was thus designated because at the time of its separation from others, the laity (*upāsaka*) and the mendicant (*bhikṣu*) participated in its congregation in large numbers. This sect originated during the second council, claimed Mahākāśyapa as its founder, had its centre at Vaishali, but later became more popular in the Andhra. It differed from the *Theravāda* not only on *Vinanya* rules but also on the nature of the Buddha, asserted that Buddha was supra-mundane (*lokottara*), that Gautama Siddhartha was only an apparition of the *Lokottara* Buddha and that *arhathood* was not the fully emancipated state. Therefore, one should aspire for the Buddhahood and nor *arhathood*. Later on it developed into *Caityakas* and *Vaitulyakas*. This only shows that the *Mahāsānghikas* and their off shoots were the real precursors of the *Mahāyāna*.

(v) Early Philosophical Concepts in Buddhisam

In the early phase of Buddhism, the master had talked of three basic doctrines, which were later acceptable to all the sub-schools of Buddhism. i.e., everything is impermanent (*sarvam anityam*), everything is substanceless (*sarvam anātmam*) and everything is painful (*sarvaṃ duḥkham*). Besides these three doctrines, Buddha had also preached the doctrine of momentariness (i.e., *sarvaṃ kṣaṇikam*). In the early realistic phase much stress was laid on the rejection of the substance as permanent and eternal. In this phase the non-substantiality of the self or soul (*pudgalanairātmya*) was widely accepted. At a later stage in the *Mādhyamika* philosophical thought the separate entity of the *dharmas* was denied (*dharmanairātmya*).

The development of the philosophical thought in Buddhism may be classified into four categories :

(i) *Sarvāstivāda* (*Vaibhāṣika*, (*Vaibhāṣika*, already discussed above)

(ii) *Sautrāntikas*

(iii) *Mādhyamikas*.

(iv) *Yogācāra / Vijñanavāda*

Out of these four above mentioned schools, the first two belong to the *Hinayāna* and are pluralistic and realistic and the rest two belong to the *Mahāyāna* and are absolute in nature.

In the following pages an attempt will be made to present a short picture of the different schools of Buddhism with regard to their respective position vis-a-vis the object, its existence and conceptual framework ; because it is not our intention to present here the detailed framework of every school of Buddhism.

(vi) Sautrāntikas

The *Sautrāntikas* believe in the direct perception (*pratyakṣa*) of the object. The earlier critical realists school of the *Śautrāntikas* admitted the reality of a moment (*kṣaṇa, svalakṣaṇa, vastusat* and *parmārthasat*) in the sense that it is independent of our knowing. It is not a manifestation or projection of consciousness or knowledge. According to the *Śautrāntika* school the two types of moments are recognized as form (*rūpa*) and consciousness (*citta*). They are of the view that we know a form by its appearance (*pratibhāsa*) only. We are never able to know the substratum (*dharmin*) of these appearances or properties (*dharma*) by our senses. According to them we directly perceive an object by our sense but infer the external object, the substratum of an appearance (*bāhyārthānumeyavāda*). While talking about epistemology, Murti observes, "The real contribution of the *Sautrāntikas* to the development of Indian thought is the discovery of the subjective - the transcendental function of the mind in constructing the empirical world".[10] It may be noted that appearance or the so called external object and the consciousness of it are found invariably together, the independence of the former cannot be maintained. Thus the blue and the consciousness of the blue are identical. According to them the existence of the external object, whose form is given in the awareness, is inferred. As a matter of fact, only the phenomenalistic form is given in our perceptual awareness. They believe in the *sārūpya* theory, which means a theory of representationalism. The essence of representationalism is that we do not directly perceive the object but are aware of our ideas only (the copies of the things or objects). The *Sautrāntikas*, however, emphatically assert that we are in direct contact with the real in the perception.

The *Sautrāntikas* derive their name from the fact that this school was against all the treatises (*śāstra*) and insisted upon returning to the "discourses" (*sutrānta*) as sources for the study of the Buddhahood.[11]

---

10. Murti, T.R.V., *Studies in Indian Thought*, Delhi, 1983, p. 275.
11. *Abhidharmakośavyākhyā*, op cit. p.15:
ये सूत्र प्रामाणिकाः न शास्त्रप्रामाणिकास्ते सौत्रान्तिकाः ।

(vii) Mādhyamikas

Nāgārjuna (150 A.D) is supposed to be the genius, who founded this school. The *Mādhyamika* school was further sub-divided into two schools the *Prāsāṅgika* represented by Buddhapālita and the *Svātāntrika* represented by Bhāvaviveka. The origin of this school can be traced to Buddha himself, who was practical minded, indifferent to metaphysics. Buddha said to Kaccāyana, "That everything exists is one extreme; that it does not exist is another. The *tathāgata* preaches the truth from the middle position (*majjhena dhamman deseti)*".[12] The works like the *Prajñāpāramitasūtras, Saddharmapuṇḍrika, Kāsyapaparivarta* and *Mahāyānasūtras* are its principal treatises. Next stage of its development is to be found in the works like *Mūlamādhyamikakārikās* of Nāgārjuna. This work has an exhaustive commentary known as *Prasannapadā* by Candrakīrti (600 A.D.). Śāntideva's *Śikṣāsamuccaya and Bodhicaryāvatāra, Śāntarakṣita's* (800 A.D.) *Tattvasaṅgraha* and Kamalaśīla's *Pañjikā* are other important treatises of this school. The *Mādhyamika* system of philosophy is famous for its dialectics. It must be observed that the critical realism of the *Sautrāntikas* led on the one hand to the dialectical absolutism and *Mādhyamika* and the idealism of the *Vijñānavāda* on the other.

(viii) The Mādhyamika Dialectics

The *Mādhyamika* school of philosophy is famous for its dialectics. As already pointed out, Buddha himself is said to be the originator of this system by saying, "That everything exists is one extreme; that it does not exist is another." In philosophy while discussing any point one is bound to take a particular position. According to this system taking any position becomes an extreme position. In this process when one takes a position there are four possible alternatives:

(i) is,
(ii) is not,
(iii) is, is not and
(iv) neither is, nor is not.

This is known as the *catuṣkoṭi* of *Mādhyamika*. This is a broader framework under which it works. As far as other philosophical issues are concerned, the *Mādhyamika* says that all these approaches may be different view points and it is

12. Majjima Nikaya, sutta 72.

necessary that among all these view points, each view point is bound to have some fault and some times these views are even contrary to each other. While criticizing these various view points, a sort of criticism is generated. This critical awareness, born out of this criticism of various view points is an awareness, which is dialectics. In simple words the criticism is dialectics and dialectics is criticism. It may be noted here that while criticizing others point of views, the *Mādhyamika* does not hold any position of his own. His only aim is to find fault with (others points of views). This is known as *reductio-ad-absurdum* (*prasaṅga*) in *Mādhyamika* dialectics.

6. The Origin and Development of the Yogācāra Literature

As far as the origin and development of the *Yogācāra* school is concerned, it is really a very difficult task to trace its exact origin because Buddha himself said nothing about it. It is a well known fact that all his teachings were oral sermons. These sermons were delivered at different places for different people keeping in view their mental standard of understanding. It is also well known that most of these sermons emerged during the course of a dialogue that was carried on between Buddha and the *bhikṣus* or the people in general. It is therefore very difficult to hold Buddha responsible for any particular philosophy.

It is only the later followers of Buddha who formulated different schools of thought from the real teachings of Buddha. Today, each one of these philosophical schools claims to be the direct descendent of the Master. Thus, we see that the origin of the *Yogācāra* philosophy is shrouded in obscurity. Amongst the earliest literature, the *Laṅkāvatārasūtra* contains some of the idealistic teachings. It contains references to *ālaya*, *manovijñāna* and to ten *bhūmis*. Another important work known as *Daśabhūmikasūtra* also contains the germs of the *Yogācāra* along with the *Gaṇḍayūhasūtra*. There is another important work *Sandhinirmocanasūtra*, which also has some germs of the later *Yogācāra* idealism. *Mahāyānaśraddhopādaśāstra* is a very important work ascribed to *Aśvaghoṣa*, the author of *Buddhacarita*. There are frequent references to such ideas as *ālayavijñāna* and *tathatā* in this work. This work is available in two Chinese versions but it is not available in Sanskrit and has not been quoted by any of the philosophical writers or commentators.

Three important authors viz., *Āryāsaṅga, Maitreyanātha* and *Vasubandhu* are generally associated with the development of *Yogācāra* school of philosophy in India. Here it may be pointed out that recent thinking in Buddhism has been forcing the scholars to accept the view that the *Maitreyanātha* was the real founder of the system. The tradition goes like this that five of his works were revealed to *Asaṅga* by *Maitreya* in *Tuṣita* heaven. Some of the scholars think that he was a mythical character rather than a historical person but some of the scholars hold different view that he was a historical person and the teacher of *Asaṅga* and he was the real founder of the *Yogācāra* school. The five works viz., (i) *Mahāyānasūtralaṅkāra,* (ii) *Madhyāntavibhāga,* (iii) *Dharmadharmātavibhaṅga,* (iv) *Uttaratantra* and (v) *Abhisamayālaṅkāra* are generally attributed to *Maitreya.*

In the development of *Yogācāra* philosophy, two brothers i.e. *Asaṅga* and *Vasubandhu* have played the major role. He, more properly *Vasubandhu Asaṅga,* was the eldest of the three brothers, who were born as the sons of a *Brahman* of the *Kauśika* family in *Puruśapura* (modern Peshawar now in Pakistan) in the extreme north of India. They probably lived in the 4th century and all the three were followers of the *Sarvāstivāda* school.

Yogācāra-Bhūmiśāstra is one of his most important works, other works. which are generally, ascribed to *Asaṅga,* are *Abhidharmasamuccaya, Mahāyānasaṅgraha, Tattvaviniścaya,* a commentary on *Uttaratantra,* and a commentary on the *Sandhinirmocanasūtra.* There are other works of *Asaṅga* which have come down to us only in the Chinese translation. They are *Mahāyānasamparigraha* translated by *Paramārtha, Prakaraṇa-Āryavācā-Mahāyānābhidharma-Saṃgiti-Śāstra* translated by Hsuan-Tsang and the commentary on the *Vajracchedikā,* translated by *Dharmagupta.* Some scholars are of the view that *Asaṅga* might have also written certain treatise works.

It has already been mentioned above that *Vasubandhu* is the key figure as far as the *Yogācāra* system is concerned and he has contributed a lot to the development of Buddhist philosophy in more than one way. He was the younger brother of *Asaṅga* and lived in the 4th century A.D. It is said about him that in the beginning he was an adherent of the *Sautrāntika* school. *Abhidharmakośa* is a remarkable work, written from the *Sarvāstivāda* point of view by him, though the work primarily concerns with the *Sautrāntika* school, but this is held in great esteem by all other philosophical schools of Buddhism. It has a famous commentary known as *Sphutārthavyākhyā* by *Yośomitra*.

Among the others, who have made significant contributions to the development of *Yogācāra* is, *Sthiramati*. He is supposed to have written commentaries on *Vasubandhu's* eight works on idealism, the most famous being the *Triṃiśikāvijñaptibhāṣya*. He has also written a commentary on *Madhyāntavibhaṅgasūtrabhāṣya*. Thus with *Sthiramati* the first phase of *Yogācāra* idealism comes to an end. It is said that here onwards the main interest of the philosophers shifted from metaphysics to logic and epistemology and there started a new school of philosophy which is generally known as *Vijñānavāda*. *Dignāga* and *Dharmakīrti* are the two important names who have contributed a lot to Buddhist logic through their works. A.K. Chatterjee observes, "This was the second phase in the development of Buddhist idealism. The first phase of pure idealism, represented by *Maitreya-Asaṅga*, *Vasubandhu* and *Sthiramati*, can be called *Yogācāra* school, the second phase of idealism-cum-critical realism, represented by *Dignāga* and *Dharmakīrti*, can be called *Vijñānavāda* school and the whole development, the *Yogācāra-Vijñānavāda*".[13]

Among the works of *Dignāga*, the most important is *Pramāṇasamuccaya*, which primarily deals with Buddhist logic. He was followed by his pupil *Dharmakīrti*, who has written an important work known as *Pramāṇavārtika* being a commentary on *Pramāṇasamuccaya*. Besides these, *Dharmakīrti* has written *Nyāyabindhu*, *Pramāṇaviniścaya*, *Hetubindu* and the *Saṃbandhaparīkṣā* and *Vādanyāya*. After this there emerged two important philosophers in the domains of Buddhist philosophy viz., *Śāntarakṣita* and *Kamulaśīla*. It is said that among the two, *Śāntarakṣita* tried to present a synthesis of the *Mādhyamika* and the *Yogācāra* systems. After this it is believed that there were no wothwhile doctrinal developments in the *Yogācāra* system.

13. Ibid. p.41.

7. Why Vijñānavāda is called Yogācāra ?

If we look into the history of Buddhism, we find that the contemporaries of Buddha were often engaged with him on the ethical questions, the explanation of the retribution and the like. It is also a well known fact that most of them were engaged in the speculative philosophy whereas Buddha was not at all interested in any speculative system of philosophy. For a philosopher at that stage universe itself was considered as an infinite process of separate elements of matter and mind appearing and disappearing without any real personalities nor any permanent substance. On the other hand Buddha was trying to find out a theoretical basis on which to establish mortality. Prior to the Buddha, the *Sāṅkhya* system of philosophy had probably presented a model of the world of analysing its elements into matters and mind. Buddha had by his hard practice of penances realised that the best means of attaining the quiescence was the profound meditation (*yoga*). Even earlier also *Patañjali's yoga* had existed where the psychology of trance plays an important role through the withdrawal of the sense-organs from their objects. It is quite certain that the form of *yoga* as it is found in Buddhism is different from the popular *yoga* of *Patañjali*. Steherebatsky says in this connection, "Very far being vulgar magic and thaumaturgy, the Buddhist teaching about *yoga* contains the following philosophical constructions which, in my opinion, the historian of philosophy can neither disregard nor fail to appreciate.... Its fundamental idea consists in the fact that the concentrated meditation induces a condition of quiescence. The meditative man is the opposite of the active man. Life is then dissected in its active elements (*saṃskāras*) with a view to be one after the other reduced to final quiescence and extinction."[14] Vasubandhu in *Abhidharmakośa* classifies *Yogācāra* into three varities: *ādikārmika*, *kṛtaparijaya* and *atikrāntamanaskāra*. From the detailed description, which follows in this text, it appears that term *Yoigācāra* was used for those persons who were interested in using *Yogic* practices for inauspicious purposes also.[15]

---

14. Stcherbatsky, *Conception of Buddhist Nirvāṇa*, Delhi, 1975, p.7.
15. Cf. *Abhidharmakośa*, op.cit. 6.9.10.11. p.896.
योगाचारस्त्रिविध उच्यते – (i) आदिकार्मिकः (ii) कृतपरिजयः (iii) अतिक्रान्तमनस्काश्च ।
.....अशुभा भावयितुकाम आदितो योगाचारः स्वाङ्गावयवे चित्तं निबध्नाति पादाङ्गुष्टे ललाटे यत्र चास्याभिरुचि ।

The basic question here is : why is this system called *Yogācāra* ? As we have seen above, the earlier phase of Buddhism was quite familiar with the *yoga* terminology. *Yogācāra* means practice of meditation. Moreover, the *Daśabhūmikasūtra* systematically proposes ten different stages (*bhūmis*) of meditation (*yoga*) for a *bodhisattva* for an overall purification.[16] In addition to this the famous work i.e. *Laṅkāvatārasūtra*[17] also induces the *boddhisattva* to follow *yoga* in order to become *Mahāyogin*. The school of *Yogācāra* deals with ideas, consciousness, mind in its works in a very extensive way. In English this school is generally known as idealism. According to this, all existence has its center and being in mind. The *Yogācāra* believes that reality is a mere idea and the same has its center in consciousness or mind. Dasgupta[18] while talking about idealism, quotes, Kant on idealism, "Thus Kant, in distinguishing other forms of idealism (mainly Berkelean) says in his Prolegomena : "Idealism consists in the assertion that there exists none but thinking entities; the other thing we think we perceive in intution being only presentation of thinking entity to which no object outside the latter can be formed to correspond." I say, on the contrary, things are given objects discoverable by our senses external to us but of what they may be in themselves we know nothing, we know only that phenomena, i.e. the presentation they produce in us as they affect our senses."

We find that the extensive usage of the *yogic* terms in the works like *Daśabhūmikasūtra* and *Laṅkāvatārasūtra* justifies the *Vijñānavāda* school to be rightly called *Yogācāra*. We have

---

16. Cf.(i) *Daśabhūmikasūtra, Vimalābhūmi*, ed. Vaidya, P.L. Darbhanga, 1967, p.16:
तस्मात् तर्ह्यस्माभिः समाभिर्निहारे सर्वाकारपरिंशोधनाभिर्निहार एव योग करणीयः ।
(ii) Ibid., 3rd *Bhūmi*, i.e., *Prabhākarī* Ibid. P.20. for different types of *dhyānas* (meditation).
17. *Lanhkāvalārasūtra*, cd., Vaidya, P.L., Darbhanga. 1963.
(i) देशयतु में भगवान् योगाभिसमयं यथा बोधिसत्त्वा महोयोगिनो भवन्ति ।
Ibid. p.34.
(ii) एभिर्महामते चतुभिर्धर्मैः समन्वागता बोधिसत्त्वा महासत्वा महायोगोगिनो भवन्ति ।
Ibid., p.34.
(iii) प्रथमोत्तोरत्तरभूमिलक्षणपरिज्ञनादधिगच्छन्ति योगिनः । Ibid., p.56.
(iv) अत्र ते महामते कायत्रयलक्षणप्रविचावबोधे योगः करणीयः । Ibid. p. 56.
(v) तस्मात्तर्हि महामते आयज्ञानलक्षणत्रययोगः करणीयः । Ibid. p.23.
(vi) अत्र महामते त्वया अन्यैश्च बोधिसत्त्वैर्महासत्त्वैयोगः करणीयः । Ibid. p.60.
18. Kant quoted by Dasgupta, S.N., *Indian Realism*, Cambridge, 1962, p.23.

also seen above that this was the first phase of this system, to which another phase i.e., *Vijñānavāda* was added subsequently. Thus the combined name of this system is properly designated as *Yogācāra / Vijñānavāda*.

8. Basic Philosophical Tenets of Yogācāra/Vijñānavāda.

Uptil now we have presented a brief survey of the background of *Yogācāra*, its origin, developments of the literature, and *Yoga*. We have also shown above as to why the earlier phase of idealism was called *Yogācāra*, to which another phase known as *Vijñanavāda* was added subsequently. It has also been pointed out above that the *Yogācāra* literature and its philosophical details emerged as its reactions against the *Mādhyamika* philosophy. We can also say that the *Yogācāra* school of the Buddhist philosophy is the significant modification of the *Mādhyamika* school. To quote Murti, "The idealism of the *Yogācāra* (*Vijñānavāda*) school has to be understood as a significant modifications of the *Mādhyamika Śūnyatā* on a constructive bases."[19]

With the emergence of *Yogācāra* school of philosophy starts the third phase of Buddhism to which we have already made a brief reference above in our survey. Before the advent of the *Yogācāra* school, the realist had been holding that the content perceived is independent of the act of perception. Moreover, the perception does not in any way change the content perceived. This process of perception can be compared with light which does not make or unmake the things upon which it shines; but merely reveals or discovers what was hidden in darkness. Before this the object was unperceived and now it is being perceived. This process only pertains to our knowledge of objects and does not in any way touch the object itself. This process of perception only reveals the objects as they are and does not construct, either wholly or in part. This was the approach adopted by the realist in relation with the empirical objects.

The *Mādhyamika* adopted altogether a different approach towards the objects of the empirical world. The *Mādhyamika* tries to refute the object from all possible view points and through its dialectics it reduces every objective to *śūnyatā*. This school is famous for its out and out rejection of all possible approaches to know the reality of the things. It firmly

---

19. Murti, T.R.V., *Central Philosophy of Buddhism*, op.cit., p.104.

asserts that the things are by nature unreal (*niḥsvabhāvā*) and so we cannot accept the reality of the things which are unreal in themselves ? By its analytical approach this school tries to prove the hollowness of the arguments in favour of the existence of the reality of the things of the world. This school declares that things are basically relative to each other and depend upon something else for their very existence. It affirms that when the things are not independent, how we can talk of their reality. By the process of dependent origination (*pratītyasamutpāda*) we reach a stage, which is called *śūnyatā*. In the simple words, it can be said that its approach to know the reality of the things is very critical and this criticism is nothing but dialectics. According to this school criticism is dialectics and dialectics is criticism. According to this system every approach to know the reality of the things is invested with some defect. In other words, we may say that these are all mere view points (*diṭhi*) and all of them have their own hollowness in them in their respective ways.

9. Perceptual Image and Conceptual Image

Coming to *Yogācāra / Vijñānavāda* tradition we find that both the above positions held by the *Sautrāntikas* and *Mādhyamikas* of realistic phase and critical phase respectively were not tenable. In order to understand the process of knowing the reality in Buddhist philosophy and more so in the *Yogācāra/Vijñānavāda* system it is essential to know what its position towards a given object of the empirical world is. Before going deeper into this process, we should first of all visualise that an object *(artha)*, i.e., any external object has two different images viz., (i) perceptual image and (ii) conceptual image. The perceptual image projects before our eyes the exact dimensional picture of the object of the external world. There is another image which is known as conceptual image. It may be pointed out that practically for all schools of philosophy of Buddhism, this conceptual image is of utmost importance as far as the question of knowing the reality is concerned. In the earlier schools of Buddhist philosophy i.e., *Sarvāstivāda* and the *Sautrāntikas*, their followers were primarily concerned with the perceptual image of the object existing in the mundane world. In case of reality or the theory of knowledge, it was the latter i.e., conceptual image which is of utmost importance to this school of *Yogācāra/Vijñānavāda*. What is the relation between the perceptual and the conceptual image ? It is presumed that there is one-to-one correspondence between a perceptual and conceptual image. Here in this context the word *'artha'* denotes an external object of the world. In other words we may say that this is truly a realism for the earlier schools of thought of Buddhism but the latter schools denied this perceptual image i.e., *'artha'* of the external world. As we shall have more occasion to see that *Vasubandhu's* major stress is on the conceptual image, which is consciousness only. It is very interesting in this connection to know as how the process of perceptual and conceptual image works through consciousness. Both these images come into existence by means of consciousness only. Herbert V. Guenther says, "Since the process of becoming conscious is not merely a reaction process to the object stimulus but also is a most active process, one in which the sensed material is used for perceiving, or what amounts to the same, where meaning accrues to form, though this dual presentation of sensed forms and given meaning is due only to the limitation, e.g. language with its linear successive order of words, while actually seeing hearing and so on are now themselves process of formulation, we are able to appreciate the statement concerning the simultaneity of sensation and formulation." This process is very nicely illustrated in the *Aṭṭhaśālinī* (III.55) thus : "Each object makes its way (into consciousness) by way two doors. Thus, a visible object simultaneously with stimulating the sensivity of the eye appears at the *manas* (*manodvāra*). The meaning is that the visible object is the irremissible condition for the activation of the unconscious (i.e., of the latent image or deposit of former similar experience). The process in respect of an audible olfactory, gestatory, and tangible object is exactly the same (as in respect to a visible object). (This process may be illustrated by a similie). Just as a bird flying through the air and alighting on the top of a tree touches a branch of the tree and its shadow strikes on the ground, the touching of the branch and the spreading of the shadow on the ground taking place simultaneously, so also the stimulation of the sensitivity of the eye by the visible object and its appearance at the subject factor (*manas*) by virtue of its ability to activate the (latent image of the object in the) consciousness takes place simultaneously. After that, the image having been selected from the unconscious continuum immediately after the process just described, and having started with attention and ended with judgement as to the visible object, a conscious perception with regard to any objective comes into existence."[20] Yuichi Kajiyama observes in connection with the perception of an external object, "When we are perceiving an external object, say a book, or when we are thinking of an idea, we are usually not conscious of the division of that cognition into three elements. The world of cognition appears at first as inseparable whole, and it is only through our logical reflection that it is divided into the three. This is the view of the *Sautrāntikas*. The *Sarvāstivāda* philosopher, however, does not believe in the reality of the whole. What is real to him is only the three components parts i.e., the instrument of cognition, the object, and the consciousness. In the case of visible perception, for example, the eyes, the colour, and consciousness or understanding of what is seen are realities but visible perception as a whole is not. In the case of cognition of an idea the mind is the instrument, the idea as object and consciousness as subject are admitted as real, but not the cognitions a whole. In this case we have to note that the mind as an organ is actually the mind at the preceding moment (*manas*) and that consciousness is the mind at present moment (*vijñāna*)."[21]

We have seen above how the position held by the earlier schools of Buddhist were not acceptable to the *Yogācāra/Vijñānavāda* system and hence they evolved their own philosophy towards the reality. Thus the basic tenets of idealism can be understood in the following way. The object is not as it appears, and cannot be of any service as far as the theory of knowledge is concerned. It is, therefore unreal, consciousness (*vijñapti*) is the sole reality. The object is only a mode of consciousness. The external appearance of the object is the transcendental illusion, because of which consciousness is bifurcated into subject-object duality. Consciousness is creative and its creativity is governed by the illusory idea of the object. The process of idealism takes place through these three strata of consciousness viz., *ālayavijñāna*, *kliṣṭa manas* and the *pravṛtti vijñāna*. Everything that exists is

---

20. *Philosophy and Psychology in the Abhidharma*, Delhi, 1974, p.27.
21. Kajiyama, Yuichi, *Buddhist Thought and Civilisation*, "Realism of the Sarvāstivāda School", (Essays in Honour of Herbert. V. Guenther on His Sixtieth Birthday) Ed. Leslie S. Kawamura and Keith Scott, Dharma Publishing, California, 1977, p.115.

exhausted into these three. They are not, however, the ultimate form of consciousness. When the object is realised to be illusory, its sublation is followed by the dissolution of the subject as well. Consciousness thus freed of the false duality of subject and object, is absolute. This is the ultimate reality, the essence of every thing (*dharmāṇāṃ dharmatā*).

As far as the historical and doctrinal development of *Yogācāra/Vijñānavāda* is concerned, it may be pointed out that the whole of the *Vijñānavāda* tradition may be divided into two catagories viz., *Āgamānuāyī Vijñānavādins and the YuktyānuyāyīVijñānavādins. Āryāsaṅga* is said to be the follower of the first tradition. According to his tradition the basic tenets of the *Vijñāvāda* may be divided into *ālayavijñāna* and *kliṣṭa manovijñāna. Vasubandhu,* the author of the *Vijñaptimātratā* is also the follower of this very tradition. The tradition represented by *Dignāga* and *Dharmakīrti* does not accept the concept of *ālayavijñāna* and they belong to the *Yuktyānuyāyī* tradition of *Vijñānavda.*

10. Āgamānuyāyaī Tradition of Vijñanavāda

Followers of the basic *Sūtras* of *ālayavijñāna* are generally known as the *Āgamānuyāyī Vijnānavādins.* While elucidiating the *ālayavijñāna* in the fifth chapter of *Ārya-sandhinirmocanasūtra* known as *Viśālamatiparipṛchhā,* the Lord said thus :

आदानविज्ञानगभीरसूक्ष्मो ओघो यथा वर्तति सर्वबीजो ।
बालान् एषो मयि न प्रकाशितो मा हैव आत्मा परिकल्पयेयुः ॥[२२]

(*Ādānavijñāna (ālayavijñāna)* is very deep and subtle and it is like the flow of the flood carrying the seeds of everything. It has not been exposed by me to the children (literally meaning the masses) so that they may not misunderstand this as self (*ātman*) and get disillusioned by it).

The concept of *ālayavijñāna* is the most important principle of the *Vijñānavādins.* This can be translated in English as store-consciousness. In this system there is the store-consciousness (*ālayavijñāna*), thought-consciousness (*manovijñāna*) and active-consciousness (*pravṛttivijñāna*). They respectively represent three stages in the development of consciousness, i.e., maturing, thinking and knowing the objects. *Vasubandhu* speaks of this concept of *ālayavijñāna* in

---

22. Quoted by Pandit Ram Shankara Tripathi in his *Vijñaptimātratāsiddhi,* Varanasi, 1977, p.21.

Triṃśikā (2.3.4) : they are namely, maturing (*vipāka*), thinking (*manana*) and representation of consciousness of object (*vijñapti-viṣayasya*). There the maturing (consciousness) is otherwise called the store-consciousness (*ālayavijñāna*) which carries the seeds of all (past experience). It has (within itself) the representation of consciousness of unknown objects and places. It is always associated with touch, attentiveness, knowledge, conception and volition.[23] *Āryāsaṅga* has elaborately explained this concept of store-consciousness (*ālayavijñāna*) in his *Yogācārabhūmi*. *Vasubandhu* has also explained it in *Triṃśikā*. In order to fully comprehend this concept of store-consciousness one has to understand four of its ancillaries, viz., (i) basis (*ālambana*), (ii) form (*ākāra*), nature (*svabhāva* or *svarūpa*) and (iv) mental states (*saṃprayuktacaitasika*). Similarly in order to understand the concept of thought consciousness (*kliṣṭamanovijñāna*) one has to understand four of its above mentioned ancillaries viz., (i) basis, (ii) form, (iii) nature and (iv) mental states.

It may be said that the *Āgamānuyāyī* tradition of *Vijñānavāda* further accepts eight consciousnesses (*vijñānas*) viz., (i) *ālayavijñāna*, (ii) *kliṣṭamanovijñāna*, (iii) *cakṣurvijñāna*, (iv) *srotravijñāna*, (v) *ghrāṇavijñāna*. (vi) *jihvāvijñāna*, (vii) *kāyavijñāna* and (viii) *manovijñāna*. According to another tradition of Buddhism these may be even reduced to six.

11. Yuktyānuyāyī Tradition of Vijñānavādins

As it has been already mentioned above that *Dignāga* and *Dharamakīrti* belong to this tradition of *Yuktyānuyāyī* of *Vijñānavāda*, which lays more stress on logic (*yukti*) rather that on scripture (*āgama*). It is interesting to note that there is no reference of the concept of store-consciousness (*ālayavijñāna*) in the works of *Dignāga* and *Dharmakīrti*. This only shows that both of them were not the supporters of this general theory of store-consciousness, otherwise they would have explained and defined *vijñāna* along with their examples. Since both of them do not accept the general theory of store-consciousness, they also do not follow the theory of *kliṣṭamanovijñāna*.

---

23. Triṃśikā, op.cit. *Kārikās* 2,3,4,.p.81.
विपाको मननाख्यश्च विज्ञप्तिविर्षयस्य च ।
तत्रालयाख्यं विज्ञानं सर्वबीजकम् ॥
असंविदितकोपादिस्थानविज्ञप्तिकं च तत् ॥
सदास्पर्शमनस्कारवित्संज्ञाचेतनान्वितम्
उपेक्षा वेदना तत्रानिवृत्ता. व्याकृतं च तत् ॥

Moreover, they reduced the above mentioned eight *vijñānas* to six in their works dealing with *vijñānavāda*. They accept the following six *vijñānas* viz., (i) *cakṣurvijñāna*, (ii) *srotravijñāna*, (iii) *ghrāṇavijñāna*, (iv) *jihvāvijñāna*, (v) *kāyavijñāna* and (vi) *manovijñāna*. They also accept the impressions (*vāsanās*) but they are not based upon the concept of store-consciousness. They are based on the concept of *manovijñāna*.

12. Common Characteristics acceptable to both the tradtions

Apart from the *Viṃśatikā* and *Triṃśikā* *Vasubandhu* has also written another important work which deals with the three natures (*tri-svabhāvanirdeśa*) of things. It is known as the doctrine of three natures (*tri-svabhāva*). The three *svabhāvas* are the following :

(i) *pariniṣpanna svabhāva* (the absolutely accomplished nature) is that state of existence in which the individual is characterised neither as a subject nor as an object.

(ii) *paratantra svabhāva* (the imagined nature) is that state of existence in which the individual is bound to see things as distinguished into subjects and objects of experience.

(iii) *parikalpita svabhāva* (the imagined nature) is that state of existence in which the individual is seen as an object or subject of experience.

Of the three natures mentioned above the (i) *pariniṣpanna* and (ii) *parikalpita* have an ontological status. The former is the absolute state of existence, while the latter is the *saṃsāric* (phenomenal) state of existence. The *paratantrasvabhāva* refers to the very act of projecting the forms of subjectivity and objectivity, which every individual in the *saṃsāric* state is bound to do. *Paratantra svabhāva* is a characteristics with which one's *saṃsāric* experience is marked and *parikalpita svabhāva* refers to the imaginary forms of subjectivity and objectivity superimposed on things.

13. Non-substantiality of the self and the dharmas (*Pudgala nairātmya* and *dharmanairātmya*)

Pudgala-nairātmya and *dharma-nairātmya* (non-substantiality of the self and the *dharmas*) are the two important concepts associated the *Hinayāna* and *Mahāyāna* respectively. The first parts in both these words have their own repective historical background. The word '*pudgala*' has its association with Jainism also apart from its usage in the Buddhist philosophy. From its occurances, both in Jainism and Buddhism, it appears that it is a sort of generic term. Another part in the second concpet i.e., *dharma-nairātmya* is *'dharma'* which is very popular in *Hinayāna* and as well as in the *Mahāyāna*. This word is capable of admitting a number of meanings but loosely translated into English language it conveys the sense of 'elements of existence'. Apart from these two words *pudgala* and *dharma*, another term i.e., *nairātmya* is associated with these two words. In the early Buddhism is used a word *'anattā'* to convey a similar idea of soullessness. Like *pudgala* this is also a generic idea of Buddhism that is sought to be understood and interpreted by several schools. We must acknowledge that the concept of *nairātmya* is often misunderstood and misinterpereted by the scholars both .ern and western. From its derived meanings it appears that they have not been able to catch the true meaning which it intends to convey.

In order to really comprehend as to why Buddha adopted an altogether different approach from the *ātmic* tradition, we should visualise the philosophical scene prevalent in those times. Previous to the emergence of Buddha on the philosophical plane of India, all philosophical systems of India except *Cārvāka* had *ātman* as a pivot of their thinking. All these philosophical systems, which believed in the existence of the *Vedas* and *Īśvara*, had built an edifice in which the concept of *ātman* was a prominent one. The concept of *ātman* was always described as permanent and eternal. Not only that, this was subsequently associated with *Brahman* (of the *Upaniṣads*). This *ātmaic* tradition had a great hold on the religious and social conditions of ancient India. It is here where Buddha got the clue to attack this concept of *ātman* itself from two sides i.e., phenomenal and the transcendental. This is the background from where he dervied his inspiration to build a philosophical system which was against the *ātmic* tradition. This background paved the way for the concept of *anattā* and *nairatmya*. *Anattā* is not truly the absence of *ātman* or soullessness. What is intended in the usage of this word is to show that Buddha believed in the denial of substance in the form of an *ātman*. He taught that there is no inner and immutable core in things and everything is in a flux. Existence for the Buddhist is momentary (*kṣaṇika*) and unique (*svalakṣaṇa*). Buddha altogether rejected the substance view of reality (*ātmavāda*) as propounded by the *Upaniṣads* and their followers. As already pointed out earlier that the concept of *anattā* or *nairātmya* is highly misunderstood by scholars. Buddha had rejected the idea of a permanent soul or self both at the phenomenal and transcendental level. What subsequently happened was that the followers of the Buddhist traditions laid major stress on the rejection of its transcendental side. In their frenzy and zeal to oppose the *Brāhmanical* tradition they totally forget to keep in view its empirical side. This may be illustrated in the following way. All the objects of the world consist of matter and form. When we look for reality, what appears is only their apparent false form whereas the objects of the world do not possess any permanent stuff and substance. It is this stuff and substance which have been denied by the Buddha. It may be emphasised here that while rejecting the notion of a permanent soul or self of *Brāhmanical* tradition, the scholars have missed this side of the phenomenal objects of the world i.e., they (objects) do not possess any permanent stuff and substance. To quote Christmas Humpharys, "In view of the gross misapprehension of this doctrine, what is basic to all schools of Buddhism, it is important to understand that Buddha never taught that there is no self or reincarnating entity, still less did he teach no SELF, in the sense of an Absolute beyond the reach of words. The Buddha taught that in none of the constitutents of the personality, the physical body, feeling, mental attributes and discriminative consciousness is there a permanent element which distuinghes that man from any other."[24]

Coming to the concept of non-substantiality of the self(*pudgalanairātmya*), it may be said that the early Buddhism had preached the five aggregates (*skandha*) apart from feeling (*vedanā*), volition (*cetanā*), name (*saṁjña*), group (*saṃkhāra*) and form (*rūpa*). It was maintained in the early Buddhism that there existed the aggregates but there was nothing like a permanent self or a soul as comprehended by the *Upaniṣads* and the philosophical traditions following them. It may be mentioned that *Vasubandhu* devotes one chapter to the discussion and refutation of the *ātma*-doctrine (*pudgalaviniṣcaya*). Basically it is a refutation or condemnation of a sub-sect of Buddhism i.e., *Vātsīputrīya* school, which accepted the *pudgala* as a sort of quasi-permanent self, neither identical with nor

24. Christmas Humpharys, *The Buddhist Way of Life*, London, 1969, p.36.

different from the mental states (*skandha*). It may be observed that *non-ātmic* tradition only distingusihes Buddhism with other systems of philosophy. Murti says, "The acceptance of the *ātman* is what divided true orthodox from the Buddhist systems. The Jainas agree with this characterisation, and sharply distinguish their view from purely modal view of the Buddhist".[25] According to *Śāntarakṣita*[26] it is the *nairātmyavāda* which distinguishes the teachings of Buddha from others.

In the later development of Buddhism i.e., *Mādhyamika* philosophy of concept of non-substantiality of the *dharmas* was widely accepted. It basically denied the separate reality of the elements (of existence). According to this, substance is unreal, a thought-construction (*vikalpa*) and the modes and attributes (associated with the thought-construction) are also unreal. The text *Viṃśatikā* says, "A characterstic (*svabhāva*), known as graspable (*grāhya*) and grasper (*grāhaka*) is only imagined by the children (*bāla*). That being imaginary, there is the absence of the substantiality of the *dharmas*". It is well known that with the emergence of the *Mādhyamika* philosophical system in Buddhism, there were radical changes in the earlier concepts. The *Mādhyamika* system reduced every phenomenal object to *śūnyatā* by applying the law of dependent origination (*pratītyasamutpāda*). As already stated earlier, all the phenomenal objects of the world are unreal in themselves, it is only for our day-to-day convenience that we have not only given them certain labels and utilitarian nomenclatures, but due to our sheer ignorance we have also associated certain functional actions with them such as graspable (*grāhya*) and grasper (*grāhaka*). Whereas as a matter of fact, none of the phenomenal objects is capable of performing any action whatsoever. It is only we, who have falsely superimposed certain functions / actions/labels/names/ utilitarian nomenclatures on them. The *Viṃśatikā* refers to this as imaginary (*parikalpita*). So all these functional actions/labels/names/nomenclatures (falsely superimposed by us on them) are imaginary, unreal and hence non-existent. It must be understood that all these i.e., lables/names/utilitarian nomenclatures/functional actions have been denied. It does

25. Murti, T.R.V., *Central Philosophy of Buddhism*, p.27.
26. Cf. *Tattva sangraha*, Vol. II ed. Dwarkadass Shastri, Varanasi, 1968, p.1061.
एतश्च सुगतस्येष्टमादौ नैरात्म्यकीर्तनात् ।
सर्वतीर्थकृतां तस्मात् स्थितो मूर्ध्नि तथागतः ।।

not mean that the objects are not there. Nowhere it is said that these objects do not exist from the *sāṃvṛtika* point of view. What is denied, is the false super imposition (as mentioned above) by us on these objects of the world. It is real import of the concept of the non-substantiality of the *dharmas* (*dharma nairātmya*). According to the *Viṃśatikā* by the non-substantiality of the self (*pudgala nairātmya*) one enters into the domain of the non-substantiality of the *dharmas* (*dharma nairātmya*) and by the non-substantiality of the *dharmas* one enters into *Nirvāṇa*.

14. The Three Vijñānas

As we have already shown above that *Yogācāra* form of idealism accepts three different types of *vijñānas* viz., (i) *ālayavijñāna*, (ii) *kliṣṭa manovijñāna* and (iii) *pravṛtti vijñāna*. We have also talked about the six different *vijñānas* connected with our six sense organs and thus we see that evolutes of *vijñāna* are infinite, and yet there are three stages of its evolution. Among these *vijñānas* the most important is the *ālayavijñāna* (store-consciousness) because it is said to contain all the seeds (*bīja*) and impressions (*vāsanās*) in itself. This *ālayavijñāna* has been compared with the flow of a vast river carrying in its stream a number of things along with it.

15. Ālayavijñāna

As already stated above, it is the *ālaya*, because it is the place/repository/receptum in which all the seeds (*bījas*) and impressions (*vāsanās*) of any *karman* whatsoever good, bad or indifferent are contained. It is called the *savra bījaka* (maturation of all the seeds). All the actions done by any individual get maturity in this *vijñāna*. It is the receptum of the impressions of past *vijñānas*, while in its own turn it gives rise to further *vijñānas* by maturing those impressions.[27] The accumulation of seeds of *vijñāna* in *ālaya* is called the *hetu pariṇāma*, while their actualisation, the *phala pariṇāma*. *Hetupariṇāma* is the development and maturity of *vāsanās* in the *ālaya*, and the *phala pariṇāma* is the merging into the existence of their respective effects. *Vāsanā* is to be understood as the motive force governing the evolutionary process.[28] It

---

27. धर्माः आलयविज्ञाने धर्मेषु च विज्ञानं तथा फलस्वभावश्च अन्योऽयं हेतुस्वभावा सर्वाः । *Mahāyāna-Abhidharma-sūtra* (quoted by A.K. Chatterjee, *The Yogācāra Idealism*, p.88).

is of two kinds; (i) *vipāka vāsanā* and (ii) *niḥṣyanda vāsanā*. *Vipākavāsanā* keeps going the stream of mental process, i.e., the continuity of the individual through the successive births. When the repercussions of previous *karmas* come to an end and death intervenes, the activity of *vipākavāsanā* forces the *ālayavijñāna* into a new stream, beginning from next birth of the individual. *Niḥṣyanda vāsanā* is the fructification of the present experiences, due to the maturity of this, the other *Vijñānas-kliṣṭa manas* and the various *pravṛttivijñānas* evolve out of the *ālaya*. *Vipākavāsanā* maintains the cycle of births; *niḥṣyanda vāsanā* supplies the content of each birth. *Pravṛttivijñāna* alone, being conscious experience proper, can lay both sorts of *vāsanās* in the *ālaya;* only a conscious experience can be good or bad and can supply the seed of future experiences. *Manovijñāna* is more or less a function ; it supplies only the *niḥṣyandavāsanā;* the force which impels the present experience.

It has already been stated above that the concept of *ālayavijñāna* is the most important in the *Yogācāra* idealism. In other words we may say that this is a sort of store-house of different kinds of consciousness. This store-house of consciousness is always associated with various types of seeds (*bījas*) and impressions (*vāsanās*). It must be also noted that the main function of *vijñāna* is its creative faculty. Whenever there is anything visible in the external world, the mind immediately links it with its equivalent *vāsanā* and tries to project or create a similar other object in the empirical world.[29] Hence it is said that the *ālaya* functions in two ways : (i) internally, i.e., consciousness appearing as the constituents of an individual, and (ii) externally as consciousness of the undifferentiated objectively (*aparicchinnākārabhājana*). Then it becomes the function of the consciousness to create an 'other' and to project it as distinct from itself. Thus the consciousness chooses an object from various indeterminate objects and creates, an 'other' and projects it as such. The beauty of this process lies in the fact that the 'other' which it has, projects

---

28. Ibid. (i) ईष्यते वासनाविद्भिः शक्तिरूपा हि वासनाः । p.88.
Ibid. (ii) ज्ञानस्यैव शक्तिमातरं वासना ।p.88.

29. *Triṃśikā*, 18-19, op.cit. p.82.
सर्वबीजं हि विज्ञानं परिणामस्तथा तथा ।
यान्त्यन्योन्यवशाद येन विकल्प. स स जायते ।।
कर्मणो वासना ग्राह्यद्वयवासनाया सह ।
क्षीणे पू र्व विपाके ऽन्यद् विपाकं जनयन्ति तत् ।।

out of itself is not known as an "other" A.K.Chatterjee observes in this connection, "The idea of the 'other' will indeed not let it rest in peace, it must be known and as soon as it is known as an 'other', it is known as a determinate other. The *ālaya* situation is inherently unstable, and yet the consciousness of a determinate other leaves its impression in the *ālaya* as *vāsanā*, which makes it impossible for the *ālaya* to be wholly determined; as one moment of the *ālaya* gets differentiated, its place to be further differentiated, so that though the *ālaya* is unstable, it can never be exhausted till the idea of objectivity itself is eradicated".[30]

It must be pointed out here that *ālayavijñāna* of the *Yogācāra* idealism bears a close similarity with the *prakṛti* of the *Sāṅkhya* system of philosophy because both these systems accept the doctrine of evolution, one from the realistic stand point, the other from the idealistic one. As the *ālayavijñāna* is the repository of all the seeds in *Yogācāra* idealism, every objective thing is traced back to the *prakṛti* in the *Sāṅkhya* system.

This *ālayavijñāna* differs from person to person. Each human being has his/her own *ālayavijñāna*. Lambert Schmithausen says, "It must be kept in mind that (at least in the "orthodox" *Yogācāra* school) *ālayavijñāna* is strictly person-bound, each living being having its own *ālayavijñāna*."[31]

16. Kliṣṭa manovijñāna

Next stage in the development of the *Yogācāra* idealism is that of *kliṣṭamanovijñāna*. We have already seen above that the *ālayavijñāna* tries to locate the objects from a series of indeterminate objects with the help of different *vāsanās* (impressions) connected with it. Now the question arises: how is that exactly to be done; because the consciousness itself is momentary, and unless its seeds are stored in the *ālaya*, its further continuity will, of its own accord, come to an end. In the initial stage the *ālaya* is replete with contents of the indeterminate objects; in the second stage there is a process of determination and the third stage is the final one when the determinate contents become final. The second stage,

30. *The Yogācāra Idealism*, p.91.
31. For a detailed study of *Ālayavijñāna*, see Lambert Schmithausen's *Ālayavijñāna* (On the Origin & The Early Development of A Central Concept of *Yogācāra* Philosophy) 2 Volumes, The International Institute for Buddhist Studies, Tokyo, 1987, p.1.

which is the intermediate stage, is associated with the mind (*manas*). This is also known as the transitional stage which is associated with the *manas*. The function of the *manas* is of intellection (*manana*) and also of categorisation of the object. This work of determinate categorisation is performed by *manas*. For an object to reach the stage of the *pravṛttivijñāna*, these three successive stages beginning from *ālayavijñāna* and the indeterminate being that of the *kliṣṭamanovijñāna* and the last being the final one i.e., *pravṛttivijñāna* all these are the successive evolutes in the development of any object whatsoever. Thus the journey of indeterminate objects in association with the *ālayavijñāna* passing through the *manas* with determination of their contents reaches the final stage at the *pravṛttivijñāna*.

17. Pravṛttivijñāna

Pravṛttivijñāna is the last stage in the development of the consciousness. In this stage one acquires the determinate awareness of the object. This stage is very important from the empiricial point of view. When this stage is reached, the previous two forms are submerged into this. In this stage one is sure about the determinate contents of the object through the consciousness. Such a consciousness is divided into six different types of consciousnesses viz., five consciousnesses connected with the five sense-organs which supply us information (or stimuli). These five are matter (*rūpa*), sound (*śabda*), smell (*gandha*), taste (*rasa*) and tactual data (*sprarṣṭvya*) and the sixth being the internal consciousness known as the *manovijñāna*. This *manovijñāna* is definitely different from the *kliṣṭsmanas*, because the two are related to two different realism. A.K.Chatterjee observes, "This *manovijñāna* is not to be confused with *kliṣṭamanas*; the latter is a transcendental function, while the former is merely the knowledge of empirical ideas."[32]

It must be pointed out that none of these three *vijiñānas* or the previously mentioned six or eight *vijñānas* are ultimate ones. It is this consciousness, which reaches this final stage starting from the *ālaya* mediated by the *manas* and culminating in the *pravṛttivijñāna* is the Reality according to the idealism of the *Yogācāra*.

---

32. *The Yogācāra Idealism*, p.106.

18. Refutation of Atomism

While rejecting the external object as unreal, *Vasubandhu* has outrightly stated that form and colour etc., cannot be exhibited in atoms in any way either singularly or in a conglomeration of them. According to him the atom itself cannot be proved.

It may be observed at the initial stage that *Vasubandhu's* refutation of an atom is based on the idea that the atomic hypothesis is untenable as far as perceptual experience of the various objects is concerned. This attempt on the part of *Vasubandhu* is mainly directed against the atomic realism of *Vaiśeṣika* system, which had earlier accepted objects of our experience as aggregates of atoms being the ultimate constituents. *Vasubandhu* is trying to hit hard the pluralism of the realists. The entire discussion is about the things in as much they become objects of our knowledge. The basic question is; in what mode the objects are known or experienced; as a single entity, or as many discrete atoms, or as aggregate of atoms. *Vasubandhu* suggests that neither of the modes form part of our experience. Presuming an object to be white or blue, we can say that whiteness or blueness of the object is ultimately associated with the object itself. If the object (white or blue) were to consist of various atoms as the ultimate constituents of the object, where one can locate whiteness or blueness in the atoms when they are separated from each other. Moreover, there is a limit upto which an object can be separated from its parts and thus we see that an atom has a magnitude and yet is composed of no further parts. The crux of the problem is the way in which the atom get combined together.

As already pointed out above, *Vasubandhu* is questioning as to what is the true mode of experiencing or knowing an object. Different schools of philosophy have presented various models for experiencing or knowing an object through our sense data. In the present case, he is referring to a specific model of the *Vaiśeṣikas,* who believe that the object is a conglomeration of different atoms joining together. Is an object experienced as a whole complete unit just as the *Vaiśeṣikas* speak of an object ? Or is it experienced as a conglomeration of different atoms ? To say this is different words, *Vasubandhu* wants to know as to where the form or colour is contained ? Is the form or colour contained in one atom, different atoms or in a conglomeration of different atoms ? When we are discussing whether the form or colour is contained in one atom or in a conglomeration of atoms, there is another allied question of the position of atoms in relation to each other. This has numerous dimensions and we shall have various occasions when the different aspects concerning atoms are gradually taken up for discussion. When we see an object, we see it through our eye consciousness, i.e., our eye sense organ perceives it. In the first instance the object is directly carried to our eye consciousness as a big (or small depending upon the size of the object) mass. In this mass there are various atoms constituting the object. Those atoms are the parts (*avayavas*) and the object is a whole (*avayavī*). At the first sight we get the perception of the whole (*avayavī*). But in this stance the various atoms also form the parts of the perception of the whole. Are all atoms constituting this (*bigger*) whole different or separate from the whole (*avayavī*) ? Such questions have been agitating the minds of different philosophers since times immemorial and each school of philosophy is trying to find out a suitable answer to this. The observation of A.K.Chatterjee is worth quoting in this regard, "It cannot be held that what is perceived in the whole, which, itself not being atomic, is yet made of atoms, since no whole can be admitted over and above the atoms or the ultimate parts. So the dilemma is: the atom is not an object of perception, yet the object of perception is nothing apart from atoms".[33] The discussion of part and the whole can be illustrated by the example of cloth and the threads. Is the cloth different from the threads ? Or the threads are different from the cloth ? Are the cloth and the threads similar ? Again to quote Chatterjee, "Nor can the object be held to be a whole of parts. If there be one universal whole of which the empirical objects are parts, then it must be asked whether the latter are identical with the whole or not. If not, they cannot be created out of the latter, being different from it, if identical with it their mutual difference cannot be maintained. If the object is a whole made up of its own parts, it must be asked what this whole (*avayavi*) is apart form its parts (*avayavas*). Where is the cloth when the threads constituting it have been separated ? How is it related to the threads ? Where does it exist ? Does it exist wholly in each of its parts or only partially so ? If the former, one part would be idenrical with the whole, and the rest superfluous. Then,

33. Chatterjee, Ashok Kumar, *The Yogācāra Idealism* p.70.

is the whole identical with the parts or different from them ? If identical, with which part ? And moreover, if it is identical with the parts, it cannot be a separate existent apart from them. But if it is something different from the parts, it cannot be related to them, like any other set of two different. Again some parts have features which have some contradictory ones. A part of the cloth is in the sun and the rest in the shade, which should be supposed to pertain to the whole ? Both cannot pertain to the same whole at the same time, for how can that be one which has opposed characteristics ? (योऽसौ विरुद्धधर्माध्यसवान् नासवेकः"[34]). *Vasubandhu* is suggesting that in any given object, the hypothesis of atomic conglomeration is highly untenable. In any given perceptual image the whole (*avayavī*) and the parts (*avayavas*) are taken together or are rather carried to your mind through the eye consciousness. So the basic question remains: which, the whole or the parts, are truly the container of the object and here too its other attributes like whiteness or blueness are also said to be considered simultaneously as to where those attributes of the whiteness or blueness lie, whether in the whole or in the parts.

The refutation of atomism has a number of dimensions. Until now, we have considered the question of whole and parts. The object in itself is a big mass. Presuming that the object or a mass is a combination of atoms joining each other at a central focal point. While refuting the atomism *Vasubandhu* has also examined the structure of a mass being constituted by the different atoms. In this process there can be two possibilities. In the case of the first possibility we have to presume that there has to be one atom in the center, to which six atoms coming from six directions would join together and thus world form a single mass. This possibility of a mass in the form of an atom being combined with six atoms from six directions is shown below with the help of a diagram :

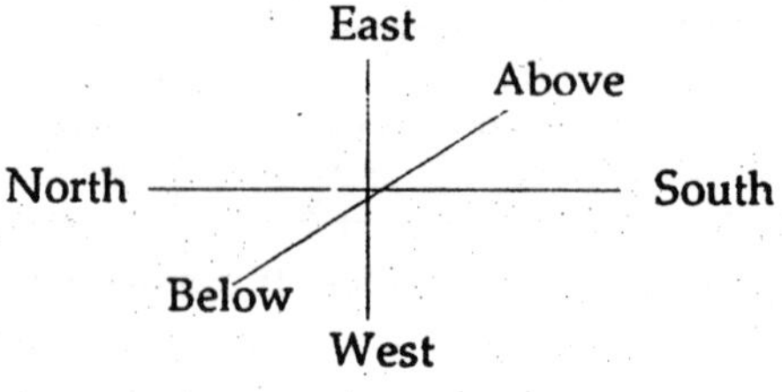

34. Ibid. pp. 63-64:

In the above diagram is shown the first position in which an atom is being joined together from six directions. Now there are two positions; (i) in the first one atoms are joining the centrally placed atom from six directions, (ii) in the second one the atoms join each other in a single direction. In the first position, when the six atoms join the centrally placed atom from six directions, then the central atom is supposed to have six parts or constituents. Thus the position of the central atom being placed in the eastern direction will not be occupied by the other atoms of the rest of the directions. With the result this atom will appear to have six indivisible parts and for such an atom containing the six constituents, it would be difficult to prove it as an indivisible single unit in the form of a substance. In the second position when the centrally placed atom is from the eastern direction, the rest of the atoms on account of not existing in different directions, in such a position, when thousands of atoms join each other (in the same direction) in such a case there would not be any extension of this atom. With the result a mass as big as that of a mountain would also be reduced to a mere atom. So in both the positions it is very difficult to prove the existence of an atom. The above examination of the atom from these two different angles reveals that both the positions are contradictory.

While making further attacks on atomism *Vasubandhu* is considering the atoms joining in the form of aggregates. He says that atoms do not join each other on account of not having any parts. *Vasubandhu* is referring here to a sub-sect of *Vaibhāṣikas* known as Kashmir *Vaibhāṣikas*. According to them the atoms join each other as aggregates. He seems to question them as far as this viability is concerned. He asks: is this joining of atom as aggregates different from the atoms themselves ? Here also the basic question remains the same : whether the mass of atom is different from the atoms or is the same ? In case you do not subscribe to the view that the atoms join each other, then whose joining can be attributed on their aggregates. He has made it clear until now that the atomic perceptual image of an object does not make any sense. It is rather endowed with numerous apparent difficulties which are contradictory in themselves. As already explained, the combination of atoms is possible only in two ways. Atoms join each other from six directions and secondly they join from one direction. In the first instance, if the atoms join each other from different directions, then the atom itself is subject to the condition of having six parts, which in itself is absurd. In the second instance, when the atoms join each other in a single direction; then the whole mass or the object is reduced to a single atom. Thus both these cases are basically untenable; because in both the cases it is very difficult to prove the very existence of an atom.

Vasubandhu has examined the atomic perceptual image of an object from the directional point of view also. Here the issue is : when one atom is supposed to come from the upper part or the eastern direction, another atom is supposed to join coming from the lower part or the western direction and thus they join together. In such a case how can you talk of the appropriateness of the unity of the atoms ? To *Vasubandhu* it is either a case of extension of a single mass in the form of an object. He is trying to base his arguments on one important fact i.e., that an atom is an indivisible unit by its very nature. In this connection any extension or extensionlessness of an atom has no significance for our purpose. If such a situation is accepted in relation to an atom, then one part of it would not have been exposed to shadow and another part to darkness. You cannot visualize any object, of which one side would be exposed to light and another to shadow. If the directional differentiation is not accepted, then how could one atom be covered by the other ? Similarly an atom does not have any other part or side where one atom becomes obstructed by the arrival of another atom. This position leads us to a point where there is no obstruction of one atom by another. All the atoms are supposed to belong to a similar place, the whole aggregate of atom would be mere atom by itself. This is very moot point which has been discussed threadbare earlier also. Such position of an atom only shows that the atom remains a single indivisible unit, of which no further dissection is possible. *Vasubandhu* argues that those who believe in the reality of an object are only pointing to out to an impossibility. Various schools of philosophy had made efforts to prove that what appears in the form of an object is nothing but a conglomeration of atoms. This is an atomic conceptualisation of the universe as suggested by *Vasubandhu's* opponents.

These are some of the bases on which *Vasubandhu* has refuted the atomism. Besides these objections against atomism he has considered this problem from the point of view of shadow and darkness.

19. Śaṅkara's Refutation of Atomism

We have presented above a brief resume of the criticism of atomism as found in the text itself. It is not only that *Vasubandhu* has criticised the atomism in his *Vijñatimātratāsiddhi* but we find that *Śaṅkara* has also vehemently criticised the atomism in his *Bhāṣya* (from 2.2.12-2.2.17). From this it appears that *Śaṅkara's* criticism of atomism is very sound and well founded. After a careful study of the whole of the context it broadly reveals that *Śaṅkara* has very minutely criticized atomism from various points of views, i.e., from the point of view parts or whole, human efforts as a cause, as combination of different elements like earth, water, fire, and air, space present between two atoms etc. It is very difficult to go into all these details here. However, we present here some of his objections against atomism. First of all it must be noted that *Śaṅkara* believes that the whole of this world is born out of atom.[35] Apart from this he presumes that even the form (*rūpa*) is born out of the atoms. As a matter of fact he himself quotes the opinion of the followers of *Kaṇāda*, who think that form (*rūpa*) is born out the atoms.[36] *Śaṅkara* has broadly classified atoms in four categories : (i) active (*pravṛttisvabhāva*), (ii) inactive (*nivṛttisvabhāva*), (iii) or both active and inactive and (iv) neither active nor inactive (*vā-anubhasvabhāva*), because no other alternative is possible.[37] *Śaṅkara* points to a situation in which the atoms seek for some effort or action for the purpose of combining together for production of a thing. As opposed to this he also points out to a situation, in which the atoms join each other due to some unknown force (*abighāta*). Thus he concludes that in that

35. *Śaṅkara Bhāṣya* on 2.2.12. Vol. II ed Dr. Soloman E.A., Delhi, 1982, p.509. Cf. एवं सर्वमिदं जगदणुभ्यः संभवति ।
36. Ibid., p.509. अणुगतेभ्यश्च रूपादिभ्यो द्व्यणुकादिगतानि रूपाणि संभवन्ति तन्तुपटन्यायेनेति काणदा मन्यन्ते ।
37. Ibid. 2.2.14. p.513. Cf. अपि चाणवः प्रवृत्तिस्वभावा वा निवृत्तिस्वभावा वोभयस्वभावा वाऽनुभयस्वभावा वाऽभ्युपगम्यन्ते अन्यतराभावात् ।

situation there is no effort done by any individual on account of absence of the body because any effort can be produced only by the individual when there is a combination of body with the mind. From all this it can be concluded that *Śaṅkara* makes a distinction between the combination of the atoms on account of human effort and the combination of the atoms just by some accident (*abhighāta*).[38] Apart from this *Śaṅkara* observes that the form (*rūpa*) of an object is a major thing (*sthūla*) and is also impermanent, e.g., the cloth is a major thing (*sthūla*) and is impermanent in relation to the pieces of the cloth (*tantu*). From this he concludes that all these pieces of cloth (*tantu)* are impermanent and thus the permanency of the atoms is not be proved at all.[39] On the basis of all these arguments *Śaṅkara* rejects the atomic theory as a cause of this universe and observes that this should not be accepted as such by the followers of the Vedic traditions because it is endowed with inconsistencies, they are against the *śruti* tradition, and because they have not been accepted by the people like *Manu* those who are desirous of bliss (*śreyas*), should not pay any heed to this.[40]

20. A Detailed Analysis of the Viṃśatikā

As far as the *Yogācāra* idealism is concerned, the work *Viṃśatikā* forming a part of the *Vijñaptimātratāsiddhi* is the most important one, because it brings out the basic tenets of the *Yogācāra* philosophy in a very lucid manner. *Vasubandhu* declares in the very first stanza that everything is mere consciousness (*vijñapti*) which means that the external objects

---

38. Ibid. p.509..
Cf. विभागावस्थानां तावदणूनां संयोगः कर्मापेक्षोऽभ्युपगन्तव्यः कर्मवतां तन्त्वदीनां संयोगदर्शनात्। कर्मणश्च कार्यत्वानिमित्तं किमप्यभ्युगन्तव्यम्। अनुभ्युपगमे निमित्ताभावान्नाणुष्वाद्यं कर्म स्यात्। अभ्युपगमेऽपि यदि प्रयत्नोऽभिधातादिर्वा यथादृष्टं किमपि कर्मणो निमित्तमभ्युपगम्येत, तस्यासंभवान्नैवाणुष्वाद्यं कर्म स्यात्। न हि तस्यामवस्थायात्मगुणः प्रयत्नः संभवति शरीराभावात् शरीरप्रतिष्ठे हि मनस्यात्मगुणः प्रयत्नो जायते।
39. Ibid. p.514. Cf. यद्धि लोके रूपादिमद्वस्तु तत्स्वाकारणापेक्षया स्थूलमनित्यं च दृष्टम्। तद्यथा पटस्तन्तूपेक्षया स्थूलोऽनित्यश्च भवति तन्त्वश्चांशूनपेक्ष्य स्थूला अनित्या भवन्ति, तथा चामी परमाणवो रूपादिमन्तैस्तैरभ्युपगम्यन्ते तस्मात्तेऽपि कारणवन्तस्तदपेक्षया स्थूलो अनित्याश्च प्राप्नुवन्ति..तदापि नावश्यं परमाणूनां नित्यत्वं साधयति।
40. Ibid. *Śaṅkara Bhāṣya* on 2.2.17. op.cit. pp.517-22.
Cf.(i) अयं तु परमाणुंकारणवादो न कैश्चिदपि शिष्टैः केनचिदप्यंशेन परिगृहीत इत्यत्यन्तमेवानादरणीयो वेदवादिभिः ॥
(ii) तदेवमसारतरतर्कसंदृब्धत्वादीश्वरकारणश्रुतिविरुद्धात्वाच्छ्रुतिप्रवणैश्च शिष्टैर्मन्वादिभिरपरिगृहीत्वादत्यन्तमेवानपेक्षाऽस्मिन् परमाणुकारणवादे कार्या श्रेयोर्थिभिरिति वाक्यशेषः।

of the empirical world have no reality at all. It is also emphasised here that the word *'vijñapti'* includes both the mind and the mental stages (*caitasika*). The second stanza is very important because it contains all the four objections raised by the realists against the *Vijñānavādins*. They believe that the external object has no reality, i.e., a consciousness is possible even without the corresponding object being present there in the external world. To this thesis of *Vasubandhu*, the realists are raising the four objections viz., (i) regulation of the observation of place, (ii) regulation of the observation of time, (iii) non-observation of the regulation of the moment series (*santānāniyama*) and (iv) functional viability (*kṛtyakriyā*). What are these objections ? Normally an experience is determined by the place and time when the object is given, it is not, however, determined with regard to the individuals enjoying it in the sense that any body present at the place and time inevitably has that experience. It is also observed that a particular experience always prompts the same kind of actions. All this is so, it is argued, because the experience corresponds to extra-mental objects. On the contrary, if such correspondence between experience and objects, is indeed, then an experience might happen at any place and time, but not necessarily to every body present, again an experience invariably leads to an action in correspondence with nature of its object, which would not happen if the experience did not have to correspond with the object. Non-observance of the regulation of the moment series (*santanāniyama*): It is presumed that blueness or yellowness of an object is to be visible to all the people present where the object is placed. If the knowledge of blueness or yellowness is not dependent upon the external objects and the observer gets the impression of blueness or yellowness in his moment series, then that blueness or yellowness should not be visible to all those present there. Just as the appearance of more than one hair in place of one hair is only visible to a man ridden with cataract in his eye and not to those (i.e., having the normal eye sight). Similarly in whose stream, i.e., moment series the cause of the impression of blueness or yellowness is present, only such a man should get the blue or yellow form and not others. But the normal practice in the mundane world is that wherever and whenever the impression of blueness or yellowness is created, all the persons present over there and at that moment shall have the impression of blueness or yellowness in the normal manner. If the external blueness or yellowness is not there; then there would not be this non-observance of the regulation of the moment series (*santanāniyama*). Here in this particular context the principle of non-observance of the regulation of the moment series means not to be present in the moment series of all but to be specially present in the moment series of a fixed or a special type of moment series. Functional viability (*kṛtyakriyā*): Here the opponents, who hold that external object is the only reality, are raising another very strong argument against the idealism of *Yogācāra* by pointing out the absence of functional viability (*kṛtyakriyā*). The argument runs like this : our experience shows that waking and dreaming stage produce two different types of results, e.g., when in a dream we take some kind of food which in reality does not satisfy our appetite whereas in the waking state that very food satisfies our appetite. In reply to these four objections raised by the realists the idealists try to support their own view point by questioning the examples of dream and hell in the stanzas starting from third upto the seventh.

After this, the realists claim that if the external objects' reality is not accepted, then this will go against the basic teaching of the Lord because the Buddha has preached the existence of the bases of knowledge (*āyatanas*) more than once. The *Vijñāavādins* say that this is true that the Buddha has talked about the bases of knowledge, but his saying so has some hidden meaning in it (*neyārtha*-hidden or secondary). *Neyārthasūtras* are those *sūtras*, which do not convey the meaning which is apparent there but that is uttered with some special purpose. There are certain *sūtras* which are like this and that is why they are secondary (*neyārtha*). After this starts a rigorous refutation of the atomism, which is put forth by the opponents in order to prove the external objects reality. Then starts a severe criticism of the theory of perception, which is advocated by the *Sautrāntikas*. After this *Vasubandhu* suggests as to how the waking and the dream experiences do not produce similar results. The opponents, who have almost exhausted their arguments against the idealists, are still not satisfied with the answers given by the *Yogācāra* idealism. They want to know how the process of death would be explained in terms of *Yogācāra/Vijñānavāda*. The *Vijñānavādins* try to explain the process of death in their own way. They hold that due to a particular consciousness of other being there is produced a transformation in other being stopping the life organ as such. By death is meant cutting off the stream of existence.[41] It may be possible that most of the modern scholars may not agree with this type of explanation of death as suggested by *Vasubandhu*. The text comes to an end by declaring that consciousness (*vijñapti*) is the only reality in the world and all the objects are mere representation of consciousness only.

21. The Meaning of Vijñaptimātra

We have seen above that the sole purpose of this text is to establish the consciousness (*vijñapti*) as the ultimate mode of reality. According to this text *Viṃśatikā*, when the consciousness (*vijñapti*) is supposed to be the only reality, this consciousness (of the mind or related with mind) projects or rather creates all the phenomena out of mind. Indirectly we may say that all the objects of the world are nothing in themselves but the creations of the mind only. The mind has infinite power stored in it in the form of store-consciousness (*ālayavijñāna*) by which it can create or project all sorts of objects in the world. There is a group of scholars who say that this process in its final shape may be designated as idealism in English language; but as soon as this word is associated with the *Yogācāra* system of philosophy, a number of difficulties arise with its usage. When the word 'idealism' is used for the *Yogācāra* system of philosophy, its western association of different types of idealism also simultaneously come to our mind viz., idealism as propounded by Berkely, Hegel and Gentile. So, we have to be very careful as far as its exact connotation is concerned for our purpose. Let us examine what meaning we propose to derive from this word 'idealism'. The word 'idealism' is formed with another word ideal, which in itself is connected with another word 'idea'. As a matter of fact, this latter word i.e., 'idea' is of much help to us in understanding the true spirit behind its usage for conveying the philosophical ideas contained in the *Yogācāra* system of philosophy. When the word idealism is used in connection with *Yogācāra* system of philosophy, its usage is intended as absolute idealism. Used in this form, this word

41. Viṃśatikā, op.cit., p.69:
Cf. जीवितेन्द्रियविरोधिनी काचिद् विक्रियोत्पद्यते, यया सभागसन्ततिच्छेदाख्यं मरणं भवतीति वेदितव्यम् ।।

tries to convey that (i) the absolute mode of reality is consciousness, mind / ideas, (ii) that the individual beings are transformations or evolutes of an absolute consciousness / mind/ ideas, (iii) that the individual beings are but illusory appearances of a monistic reality. Basically what it tries to convey is that the whole of this phenomena can be reduced to mere ideas, on which by our sheer ignorance we have superimposed the relationship of subjectivity and objectivity, whereas mere ideas are just not capable of conveying the subjectivity and objectivity associated with different objects of the world. This dualism of subjectivity and objectivity (as superimposed by us on the phenomena) is not at all intended to be conveyed by this usage of the word idealism. Thus dualism between graspable (*grāhya*) and grasper (*grāhaka*) is merely a mental construction (*parikalpita*) and that it is merely non-existent.[42] So bereft of this subjectivity and objectivity all the objects of the world are reduced to mere ideas and it is in this restricted sense that the word idealism is used to convey the philosophy of *Yogācāra* where consciousness is the only reality. It is the usage of the word 'idealism' with which we are primarily concerned. There is a group of scholars who prefers this *Yogācāra* system of philosophy to designate it with the word idealism and A.K.Chatterjee is the foremost among them.[43] It must also be noted here that when these scholars use this word idealism in connection with the *Yogācāra* philosophy, their aim is also to use the term in the absolute sense viz., they hold that the consciusness (*vijñapti*) is the ultimate mode of reality as far as the *sāṃsāric* experience is concerned meaning thereby that our mudane experience shows that the phenomenon is nothing but a mere representation of consciousness. A.K. Chatterjee,[44] Stcherbatsky,[45] C.D. Sharma,[46] P.T. Raju,[47] S.N.Dasgupta[48] are among those

---

42. *Madhyānta-vibhāga-kārikā*, 1.2. edited, Pandey, R.C. Delhi, 1971, p.9.
 द्वयं तत्र न विद्यते ।

43. Chatterjee; A.K., *The Yogācāra Idealism*, Delhi, 1975.
44. (i) Chatterjee, A.K. *Readings on Yogācāra Buddhism, Benaras*, 1970, p.31. (ii) Ibid. *The Yogācāra Idealism*, Delhi, 1975, p.87.
45. Stcherbatsky, *Madhyānta-vibhāga, Discourse on Discrimination Between Middle and Extremes*, Calcutta, 1971, p.8.
46. Sharma, C.D., *A Critical Survey of Indian Philosophy*, Delhi, 1964, p.117.
47. Raju, P.T., *Idealistic Thought of India*, New York, 1973, p.269.
48. Dasgupta, S.N., *Indian Realism*, Cambridge, 1962, pp. 119-20.

scholars, who unanimously accept *Vijñaptimātratā* or *prajñaptimātra or citta-mātratā* as the *Yogācārins'* description of the absolute, undefiled, undifferentiated, non-dual, transcendental, true, ultimate, permanent, unchanging, eternal, supramundane and unthinkable Reality. They also uquate it with *parinispannasvabhāva* or *Nirvāṇa* or Pure Consciousness or *dharmadhātu* or *dharmakāya*.

We have stated above that most scholars call the *Yogācāra* system of philosophy as idealism and we have shown how in a restricted sense this word is used. But there is another scholar viz., Thomas A. Kochumuttom who disagres with this view saying, "I do not see any reason whatsoever why the *Yogācāra* system, especially as it is found in *Vasubandhu's* writings, should be described as idealism. *Vasubandhu* spares no effort in making it clear that reality as such (*yathābhūta*) cannot be described at all in terms of consciousness (*vijñāna*). Then how is it that the *Yogācāra* system is to be regarded as an idealism" ?[49] On the other hand Kochumuttom holds that is better to call the *Yogācāra* system as realistic pluralism. He observes, "But I maintain that the entire system, when understood in terms of realistic pluralism makes better sense and that, even those passages which apparently support idealistic monism, have to be interpreted in according with realistic pluralism. By realistic pluralism I mean a theory that recognizes a plurality of beings which really exist and operate independent of each other. It positively holds that individuals are real as well as mutually independent beings."[50] Kochumuttom is again of the view, "But not even once in the four *Yogācāra* works I am studying has the term *Vijñapti* been used to describe the absolute state of reality, nor is there any indication that the final state of existence has to be defined in terms of Vijñāna".[51]

We have seen that there are two different approaches to study and interpret *Yogācāra/Vijñnavāda*. One group of scholars is of the opinion that this school of philosophy should be interpreted as idealism in the absolute sense. When this type of interpretation is intended, what is implied in this approach

49. Thomas, A. Kochumuttom, *A Buddhist Doctrine of Experience*. op.cit. p.198. (Cf. His analysis of *Madhyānta-vibhaga-kārikā* 1.4 pp. 45 ff. and the 1.15.16 pp.75.ff).
50. Ibid. p.1.
51. Ibid. p.6.

is that according to them this absolute idealism is used in the ontological sense. When the text of *Viṃśatikā* declares that *vijñāna* is the final representation of consciousness, which is nothing but a mere mental construction; we are led to believe that the whole of the phenomena is a mere projection of our mind. The approach reveals that all our social relation and experiences are to be covered under the garb of *vijñāna* and the whole of the social structure also is to be treated as a mere representation of consciousness. Interpreted in this way the consciousness plays a major role in this process and creates everything out of itself. That is the reason why the text starts with certain basic assumptions of system in which dream experiences are treated as authoritative saying that there can be consciousness even though there may not be any corresponding object being present in the dream. At one place in the text *Vasubandhu* even compares the whole of the *saṃasāric* experience with a dream. It appears that *Vasubandhu* suggests that the dream experience is to be taken only as model towards understanding the entire *saṃsāric* experience. Everybody knows that the objects experienced in dreams are not real, but only mental images. But one comes to realise it only when one wakes up from sleep. *Vasubandhu* says :

एवं वितथविकल्पाभ्यासवासनानिद्रया प्रसुप्तो लोकः
स्वप्न इवाभूतमर्थं पश्यन्‌प्रबुद्धस्तदभावं यथावन्नावगच्छति ।

In the above passage there is a clear indication to the fact that the world is fast asleep and having different impressions (*vāsanas*). Moreover, the world is endowed with a vast stretched mental constructs (*vitathavikalpa*). Again *Vasubandhu* uses two worlds in this passage i.e., *'abhutam'* and *'artham'* which mean non-existent object. Now if, we concentrate on these two words only, we can very easily grasp the real import of the *Yogācāra/Vijñānavāda* as propounded by *Vasubandhu* in *Viṃśatikā*. What *Vasubandhu* wants to convey to us is this : the object is really non-existent in the world, it is only through our mental creation that we try to give expression to these words having the different connotations. To reinforce these two words *Vasubandhu* uses another word i.e., *'abhāvam'* (absence). Here he means to say that these words have no meaning of their own and as far as meaning is concerned, the world is free to put any meaning in them according to its own choice. Indirectly this very thing has been hinted at in this very manner in which *Vasubandhu* frequently uses this phrase in most of his works i.e., *'grāhya-grāhyakabhāvena virahitatā'* (absence of the grasper and graspable distinction, Cf. *Madhyānta-vibhāga - Kārikā-bhāṣya*, 1.2). In this very passage *Vasubandhu* uses another similar term as used in *Viṃśatikā* i.e., *abhūtaparikalpasya*.[52] Here also the term *'abhūta'* is very significant in the sense that the object is non-existent and is an imaginary one (*parikalpasya*). *Vasubandhu* makes it unquestionably clear that the non-existent and imaginary objects are bereft of any graspable and grasper power, which indirectly turns out to be stage, similar to that of the *Mādhyamika* position viz., *śunyatā* (emptiness or void). This only shows that all the objects (*artha*) of the empirical world do not have any reality in them. They are bereft of any *dharma* in them. It is only our mind which puts different labels, meanings, usages and other utilitarian meanings in them. This is indirectly known as a *vikalpa* (mental constructs). There is another approach to understand the *Yogācārya* system of philosophy viz., realistic pluralism. In this approach all the individual beings are transformations or evolutes of an absolute consciousness/mind/idea and the individual beings are but illusory appearances of a monistic reality. In other words in this approach there is a plurality of beings. We have already mentioned above that Thomas K. Kochumuttom[53] is the chief exponent of this theory. When we study the text *Viṃśatikā*, we find that *Vasubandhu*[54] appears to hold a similar views. From the study of the *Viṃśatikā* it becomes quite clear that *Vasubandhu* intends to build up a social structure based on the inter-relations between different individuals. It is quite apparent that this was not possible without presuming the plurality of beings. Some portions of *Viṃśatikā* also support this assumption of plurality of beings where *Vasubandhu*[55] talks of different individuals affecting the minds of other people in the society. He even tries to explain the phenomena of death due to the consciousness of others.[56] Kochumuttom

---

52. Cf. *Madhyānta-vibhāga-kārikā-bhāṣya*, 1.2, op.cit. p.9.
शून्यता तस्य अभूत-परिकल्पस्य ग्राह्यग्राहकभावेन विरहितता ।
53. *A Buddhist Doctrine of Experience*, op.cit. pp.1-3.
54. Cf. यथा तन्निरभिलाप्येनात्मा बुद्धानां गोचरः ।
55. Cf. *Viṃśatikā* 18. op.cit. p.65.
सर्वेषां हि सत्वानामन्योऽन्यविज्ञप्त्याधिपत्येन, मिथो विज्ञप्ते र्नियभो भवति यथायोगम् । अतः सन्तानान्तरविज्ञप्तिविशेषात् सन्तानान्तरे विज्ञप्तिर्विशेष उत्पद्यते, नार्थविशेषात् ।
56. Ibid.19.
मरणं परविज्ञप्तिविशेषाद् विक्रिया यथा ।

says, "Again *Vasubandhu* seems to believe that phenomenal world is an interplay of such minds, and that representations issuing from one mind can act on those issuing from other minds, the real nature of the individuals still unaffected."[57] All these examples only suggest that there is an overall consciounsess (*vijñapti*) which is projected in all the objects of the world, the objects themselves being unreal; there is basically a plurality of human beings. In a broader social frame-work *Vasubandhu* shows how people influence each other, and how their character is affected by mutual friendship etc. This is possible only when we admit that all the different human beings are really existing. All this shows that in a society there are various individuals interacting and influencing each other.

An attempt has been made in the above lines to streamline the two basic approaches to understand and interpret the *Yogācāra/Vijñānavāda* system, viz., (i) idealism and (ii) realistic pluralism. As stated above, idealism is used to convey the ideas connected with our consciusness and mind in a very restricted sense. When we talk of idealism to convey the philosophical ideas contained in the *Yogācāra* system, this term does not show as what shall be the relative position of the different individuals beings in a society. In the idealism everything in this phenomenal world is supposed to be a mental creation of the consciousness (*vijnapti*). The consciousness is so powerful enough to create out of itself. The world in its usual manner tries to put different nomenclatures, labels, utilitarian meanings and usages in those different words (in the form of receptacle words) by means of mental constructs (*vikalpa*). We may say that all these are incapable of conveying any sense and they are mere ideas. All the objects of the phenomenal world are really non-existent (*abhūta*) in themselves and are thus unreal. It is only the consciousness which is real and when associated with these objects, is capable of conveying certain sense according to a set of accepted meaning as such. Thus the term '*idealism*' tries to explain the whole process of creating or projecting the ideas connected with the consciousness (*vijñapti*) in a systematic manner. The other term i.e., *realistic pluralism* is also used in connection with the *Yogācāra* philosophy. The main purpose of its usage for conveying the *Yogācāra* philosophy seems to put forth before

57. Ibid. pp.192-193.

the world a model of the society in which all human beings are really existent and they are inter-acting and influencing each other in a very broader manner. *Vasubandhu* is trying to show to us that the entire society is governed by the social mental frame work of the different individuals viz., consciousness and this is in a very tacit manner affecting the individuals in the society. Otherwise *Vasubandhu*[58] says that the real nature of the individuals is ineffiable, inaccessible and incommunicable. But in their phenomenal nature they are, and act like individual stream of mental energy, which can influence and affect each other. According to the realistic pluralism, *Vasubandhu* says, it is even possible to explain the phenomena of death, which can be caused by the effect of their minds consciousness.[59] It may also be noted that *Vasubandhu* has quoted some of the scriptural stories to show that the mental power is really very effective on the phenomenal level and even in affecting punishment to others by sheer means of mental power. All this reveals that *Vasubandhu* by creating a system of realistic pluralism is trying to exhibit to the world the effective power of the consciousness (*vijñapti*). In other words it may be argued that the purpose of this type of exercise on the part of *Vasubandhu* is to show that the effect may be produced somewhere else, physically on the body of some human beings, the cause of which is stored in the consciousness of certain other individuals. This indirectly suggests that the actions are possible even when there are no physical causes apparently available for them at the empirical plane. This in itself proves that all the objects and actions associated with them are unreal because it is we who are associating those empirical objects with certain actions – this has been very ably demonstrated by *Vasubandhu* when he says that there is no graspable and grasping power in the objects of the world.[60] Kochumuttom observes, "It may be recalled that Vasubandhu positively defended the idea that minds can influence each other, that the freedom of mind determines the moral worth actions, and that minds can cause harm to each other."[61] It may be concluded that both these

58. (i) Cf. *Viṃśatikā*, 10. न त्वेनभिलाप्येनात्मना यो बुद्धानां विषय इति ।
(ii) Ibid. 21. Cf. यथा तन्निरभिलाप्येनात्मना बुद्धानां गोचरः ।
59. Ibid. 19. Cf. मरणं परविज्ञप्तिविशेषाद विक्रिया यथा ।
60. Cf. *Madhyānta-vibhāga-kārikā-bhṣya* 1.2. op.cit. p.9.
शून्यता तस्य अभूत-परिकल्पस्य-ग्राह्यग्राहकभावेन विरहितता ।
61. *A Buddhist Doctrine of Experience*, p.194.

approaches to understand and interpret the *Yogācāra/Vijñnavāda* philosophy in terms of idealism and realistic pluralism (plurality of individuals) are justified in their limited sense of the terms. We have already shown above how each one of them is useful for our understanding.

22. Significance of the Suffix 'tā'

Having surveyed the two approaches, which can be adopted for understanding and interpreting the *Yogācāra/Vijñnavāda* philosophy, it is time we should concentrate on the meaning of the term '*Vijñaptimātratā*'. It may be pointed out that in the works of *Vasubandhu,* two other terms i.e., *prajñaptimātratā* or *cittamātratā* are used synonymously. They are also used as synonyms in the works of *Vasubandhu.* They are usually translated as follows :

Vijñaptimātra/Prajñaptimātra = mere consciousness/representation only *Cittamātra* = mind only

As we have already stated above that *vijñapti* means consciousnness and *Vasubandhu* has said in the beginning of the text that these four words i.e., *citta* (*mind*), *manas* (*mind*), *vijñana* and *vijñapti* (representation of consciousness) are used as synonyms. He has mentioned there that in this context the usage of the word *citta'* is intended alongwith the mental stages (*caitasikas*) and by using the word '*mātra*' (mere) *Vasubandhu* means that the term 'mere' indicates the exclusion of the external objects. So the meaning of the term '*vijñaptimātra*', would be a theory of mere representation of consciousness or thought or mind according to which all the phenomenal objects are to be treated in the realm of one's own *saṃsāric* experience as mere represntation of consciousness or the projection of the mental constructs (*vikalpa*). When this term '*vijñaptimātratā*' is used, it means a state of *Nirvāṇa,* which is same as suchness (*tathatā*) and in which one realises that what one experiences in the state of *saṃsāra* is a mere representation fo consciousness. It may mean a state in which one realises the fact that the contents of one's own *saṃsāric* experience are mere representation of consciousness. What is the purpose of adding the suffix '*tā*' with *vijñaptimātra* ? From the study of three usages of the suffix '*tā*' in the *Mādhyamika* and *Yogācāra* traditions (i.e., the usage of such terms like *śūnyatā, tathatā, rahitatā* and *dharmatā*) it can be shown that the suffix '*tā*' when added to any such terms like *dharmatā, śūnyatā* or *vijñaptimātra,* the term is used to show the state of

Nirvāṇa. In other words, the function of the suffix *'tā'* is to indicate the state to be realised. A question arises here : how does this happen ? A suitable answer to this question has been suggested by *Vasubandhu* in *Triṃśikā* where he says, "Whatever mental constructs we build (in the world), it is all a mere transformation of consciousness (*vijñānapariṇāma*). Whatever exists, is not there in reality; therefore everything is mere consciousness only." [62] We have already shown above that this consciousness is always about some object but in reality this is again without any object and thus there is no external object. The commentator *Sthiramati* makes an interesting remark in this connection and he says that one gets an impression a picture of something without an object being present there.[63] This clearly shows that this is nothing but a mental image of an object. The consciousness is always without any basis having for itself as an object and gets matured by its seeds and whatever consciousness appears in the form etc., this appearance of forms etc., does not necessarily project an object. Now this stage gives a false impression that there is a perception of an object; but in reality one gets the non-perception of (*anupalabdhi*) of the object.[64] Even a famous text like *Madhyānta-vibhāga-kārikā-bhāṣya* visulises such a stage where mere consciousness itself becomes non-perceptive in itself. The whole context runs like this : representation of consciousness (*vijñapti-mātra-upalabhadhi*), there arises non-perception of an object (*artha-anupalabdhi*). Depending upon the non-perception of the object, there arises the non-perceptionn of the mere representation of consciousness. Thus one enters (or understands), the unrealistic charactertics of graspable and grasper.[65] There is nothing

---

62. *Triṃśikā*, 17, ed Ram Shankar Tripathi, Varanasi, 1972, p.82.
Cf. विज्ञानपरिणामोऽयं विकल्पो यद् विकल्प्यते ।
तेन तन्नस्ति तेनेदं संर्वं विज्ञप्तिमात्रकम् ।।
63. Sthiramati describes this process as *citrikaraṇa* making a picture. Sthiramati on *Triṃśikā*, op.cit. 27 Ibid. p.347.
Cf. विज्ञप्तिमात्रमेवेदम् अर्थरहितं न बाह्योऽर्थोऽस्ति एवमुपलभ्यतो
ग्रहणतः चित्रीकरणत इत्यर्थः ।
64. *Madhyāntavibhāgakārikābhāṣya ṭīkā* 1.4 *Madhyānatavibhāga śāstra*. p.20. Cf.
इदं विज्ञप्तिमात्रमालम्बनार्थरहितं स्वबीजपरिकात् रूपाद्याभासं विज्ञानं
प्रवर्तते, न तु रूपादिकोऽर्थोऽसत्यीत्येवं ग्राहकोपलब्धिं निश्चित्य ग्राह्यानुपलब्धिं प्रविशति ।
65. M.V.K.B. 17 Ibid. p.20
Cf. विज्ञप्तिमात्रोपलब्धिं निश्रित्यर्थाऽनुपलब्धिर्जायिते ।
अर्थाऽनुपलब्धिं निचित्य विज्ञप्तिमात्रस्याप्यनुपलब्धिर्जायिते एवमसल्लक्षणं
ग्राह्यग्राहकयोः प्रविशति ।

which can be construed as graspable outside the purview of consciousness. It is the mind which understands (or gets into it) the absence of the graspable through the power of the mere consciousness; through the power of the absence of the graspable (*grāhyābhāvabalena*) one gets even the absence of the mere representation of the consciousness.[66] Here in this context the text seems to point out to a stage of representation of consciousness which might be empty itself and which can be compared with the stage of *śūnyatā* (emptiness) because the whole of the development of idealism is nothing but a very significant improvement of the *Mādhyamika* school in a very consctuctive way. Murti observes, "The Idealism of the *Yogācāra (Vijñānavāda)* school has to be understood as a significant modification of the *Mādhyamika śūnyatā* on a constructive basis".[67]

On the basis of the analysis of the term *Vijñaptimātra*, as it appears in various allied works of *Vasubandhu*, it can be concluded that the term i.e., *Vijñaptimātra* stands for a state of experience of objects of the empirical world, in which the passion for a subject-object distinction is not totally given up. It must also be clearly understood here that in the works of *Vasubandhu* this term represents more of an epistemological theory rather than an absolute mode of reality.[68] As soon as this passion for this two-fold (*grāhya dvaya*), i.e., subjectivity and objectivity is totally given up, one reaches a stage of realisation, that consciousness is the only reality in the world and all the different objects of the world are merely just assuming the various names and forms under the garb of false nomenclatures, labels and utilitarian means of usage. A stage slightly higher than this is equal to *Nirvāṇa*, which is same as suchness (*tathatā*). The *Triṃśika* alludes to a similar situation in stanzas 26, 27 and 28 :

As long as consciousness does not abide

---

66. Ibid. 1.7 p.22.
Cf. यथा न विज्ञानाद् बहिः परिकल्पितं ग्राह्यमस्तीति विज्ञप्तिमात्रताबलेन मनो ग्राह्याभावं प्रविशति, तथा ग्राह्याभावबलेन विज्ञप्तिमात्रस्याप्यभावं प्रतिपाद्यते ।
67. Murti. T.R.V., *Central Philosophy of Buddhism*, p.104
68. Cf. Suzuki, D.T. *Studies in the Lankāvatārasūtra*, London, 1972, p.280. ("The philosophy, if any their is any such in the Laṅkāvātara is ontology and not epistemology whereas the doctrine of Vijñaptimātratā is epistemology").

In *Vijñaptimātratā*,
The attachment to the two fold grasping
Will not cease to operate. (26)
One does not abide in it (*vijñaptimātratā*)
Just on account of the (theoretical) perception
That all this is *Vijñaptimātra*,
If one places (sees) something before oneself (27)
One does not abide in *Vijñaptimātra*
When does not perceive also a supporting
Consciousness,
For, the graspable objects being absent
There cannot either be the grasping of that
Namely, the grasping of the supporting
Consciousness (28).
(Translation, Kochumuttom)

We have tried to present a brief introduction to the development of the *Yogācāra/Vijñananavāda* idealism. The main purpose of this introduction is to study the *Yogācāra* idealism from various point of views, which we have dealt with extensively in the above pages. The *Yogācāra/Vijñānavāda* idealism is a very wide field and many more aspects can also be added to this introduction. In order to avoid unnecessary increase in the volume of the book, let us conclude this introduction by quoting *Vasubandhu* "This treatise on the theory of mere representation of consciousness has been composed by me according to my ability. It is not possible, however, to discuss this theory in all its aspects because it is known only to an enlightened one."[69]

---

69. *Viṃśatikā* 22. विज्ञप्तिमात्रतासिद्धिः स्वशक्तिसदृशी मया ।
कृतयं सर्वथा सा तु न चिन्त्या । बुद्धगोचरः ॥

PART II

नमो मञ्जुश्रिये

विंशतिका

(Viṃśatikā)

विज्ञप्तिमात्रतासिद्धिः

(Vijñapatimātratāsiddhiḥ)

स्ववृत्तिसहिता

(With the auto - commentary)

महायाने त्रैधातुकं विज्ञप्तिमात्रं व्यवस्थाप्यते " चित्तमात्रम्, भो जिनपुत्राः यदुत त्रैधातुकम्" इति सूत्रात्। चित्तं मनो विज्ञानं विज्ञप्तिश्चेति पर्यायाः । चित्तमत्र ससम्प्रयोगमभिप्रेतम् । मात्र-मित्यर्थप्रतिषेधार्थम् ।

"O, the sons of the Jina, whatever is said to belong to the three worlds is a mere representation of consciousness" - this according to the *sūtra* (aphorism), in the Mahāyāna whatever belongs to the three worlds has been established as mere representation of consciousness. Consciousness, mind, *Vijñāna* and *Vijñapti* are synonyms. Here mind is used (to convey) alongwith it associates. The term 'mere' is used for the exclusion of external object (*artha*)."

Vasubandhu starts his auto-commentary (*svavṛtti*) by quoting a well-known passage from *Daśabhūmikasūtra*. There is a controversy with regard to the reference of this *sūtra*. The commentators like *Vinītadeva* have not said anything specifically in this regard whereas *Bhavāviveka* and *Candrakīrti* while criticizing *Vijñānavāda* have accepted this *sūtra* belonging to *Daśabhūmikasūtra*. Besides this Tibetan scholars like Chonkapa Suman Kīrti have also accepted this as coming from *Daśabhūmikasūtra*. But this *sūtra*, as used by Vasubandhu in the commentary, is not traceable in the extant *Daśabhūmikasūtra*. In the present form of the *Daśabhūmikasūtra*, the vocative, *bho! Jinapūtrāḥ*, is not available whereas the rest of the *sūtra*, i.e., *cittamātraṃ yad idaṃ traidhātukam*, is available. The *Daśabhūmikasūtra* is not independently available *sūtra*; but this is the 31st appendix of the *Buddhāvatansaka*. A *Siṁhali* scholar named Pṛthavibandhu has also written a commentary on it. In the original Tibetan the translation of the *sūtra* and the commentary are not available. Among all the doctrines of the Buddha, translated into Tibetan, there is no other *Daśabhūmikasūtra* available extant. It is propable that there might have been some other *Daśabhūmikasūtra* in Sanskrit, which might have the vocative, *'bho! jinapūtrāḥ'* - and the same might not have been translated into Tibetan. From the study of the Candrakīrti's *Madhymakavatārabhāṣya* it appears that this present *sūtra* forms part of the *Buddhāvatansaka*. Janice Dean Willis says with regard to this *sūtra* "This passage has been commented upon by numerous Buddhist *doctors* of the *Mahāyāna*, both *Mādhyamika* and *Yogācāra*, throughout its history. The context of this passage at first glance seems mainly to be philosophical. In fact the quotation is centred within a discussion of the Buddhist theory of "dependent origination" (*pratītyasamutpāda*). The standard Mādhyamika interpretation of the passage is that the phrase does not deny external entities, but emphasizes that mere mind (or thought) conventially (*saṃvṛtitas*) creates the external entities. On the other hand, it is commenly held by *Mādhyamika* theorists as well many modern day scholars that for the *Yogācāra* it means the denial of all external entities of course, on the face it, an idealistic interpretation of this passage does not seem particularly strange."[1] As far as meaning, the grammatical formation and the concept is concerned, the following observation of Thomas A, Kochumuttom are worth quoting. He says, "The term *'traidhātukam'* is an adjective 'belonging to the three worlds'[2] and whereas C.H. Hamilton[3] regards this term as a substantive meaning 'The three worlds'." According to Kochumuttom this being adjective should qualify a noun or nouns, which the reader has to supply.

Mahāyāne : The whole of Buddhism is divided into *Hīnayāna* and *Mahāyāna*. What is the meanings of a *yāna*.? It may be explained as: (i) *yāti anena iti, yānam* (a vehicle by which one goes), (ii) *yāti asmin iti yānam* (a vehicle in which people go); this the term *'Mahāyāna'* denotes a bigger vehicle.The main aim of *Hīnayāna* was to obtain the *arhathood*

---

1. Willis, Janice Dean, *On knowing Reality* (The Tattvārtha Chapter of Asaṅg's Bodhisattvābhūmi), Delhi, 1982, pp.26-27.
2. Kochumuttom Thomas A, *A Buddhist Doctrine of Experience,* Delhi, 1982, p.166.
3. Hamilton, C.H. Wei Shih Er Shih Lun or The Treatise in Twenty stanzas on Representation only, New Haven; American Oriental Society, 1938, p.19.

at the level of an individual, which was considered to be a selfish approach. The purpose of *Mahāyāna* is to obtain the status of the *bodhisattva* for all the human beings of the world. The term *bodhisattva* is also sometimes used in conjunction with *yāna* in the form of *bodhisattvayāna*. *Mahāyāna* is also equated with *bodhisattvayāna*. The vehile of *bodhisattva* (the path and the fruit of thereof) is supposed to be bigger because this is superior to other *śrāvakas* and *yānas*. In the *śrāvakayāna* and other *yānas* one gets all the defilements removed by obtaining the knowledge of *pudgalanairātmya* (non-substantiality of a *pudgala*) but in the *bodhisattvayāna* by obtaining the knowledge of *pudgalanairātmya* and *dharmanairātmya* (non-substantiality of *pudgala* and *dharma*, one gets removed the ignorance of reality due to passion (*kleśāvaraṇa*) and the ignorance of the true nature of consciousness (*jñeyāvaraṇa*).

Traidhātukam : kamādhātu, rūpadhātu and *arūpadhātu* are collectively designated as *traidhātukam*. The term *'dhātu'* frequently used in Buddhist philosophy is from skt. root *'dhā'* ..*ning 'to hold' or to bear,' thus dhātu* meaning 'holder or bearer'. *Dhātus* are the bases and active agents of the different kinds of consciousness. They denote collectively both passive and active agencies. The passive agencies are the six sense organs and the six objects. Because the instruments require some active agents, this want is supplied by the six kinds of consciousness, e.g., the sense organ of eye is an agency of consciousness, it perceives an object; for instance, a chair, the chair and the eye are the two passive agencies of our consciousness; but the consciousness itself, the *cakṣurvijñāna* is the active agent of our mental operation in this particular instance. Therefore, the Buddhist psychologist avers that the six *vijñānas* are the *'dhātus'* or the 'bearers' of their own charactertics. Thus the six sense organs, the six sense objects and the six *vijñānas* make up the eighteen *'dhātus'*.

The term *'kāmadhātu'* includes the beings which are born of egg (*aṇḍaja*), of womb (*jarāyuja*), of moisture (*saṁsvedaja*) and spontaneous (*upapāduka* beings). At this very inception, the beings of the *kāmadhātu* (except the *upapādaka*) possess only two *indriyas*, viz., *kāya* and *jīvitendriya*. But among the *upapāduka* (spontaneous) beings, the *prāthamakalpikas* possess six *indriyas* (eye, ear, nose, tongue, body and vitality), gods possess seven *indriyas* and the hellish beings possess eight *indriyas*. All other *indriyas* (except the last three *indriyas*) appear here gradually. Thus in the *kārmadhātu* only 19 *indriyas* appear.

In the domain of the *rūpadhātu,* however, beings have at the very inception six *indriyas,* viz., *cakṣus* etc. five sense organs and *jīvita.* Other *indriyas* with the exception of the last three pure *indriyas* together with *strīndriya, puruṣendriya, duḥkha* and *daurmanasyendriya* appear here gradually.

In the domain of *arūpadhātu,* again beings have at the very inception one are *indriya,* i.e., *jīvita.* Other seven *indriyas* viz., *śraddhā* etc., five moral *indriyas* together with *manas* and *upekṣā* appear here gradually. Cf.

कामाप्तममलं हित्वा रूपाप्तं स्त्रीपुमिन्द्रिये ।
दुःखे च हित्वारूपाख्यप्तं सुखे चापोह्य रुचि च ।
मनोवित्तित्रयं त्रेधा द्विहेया दुर्मनस्कता ।
नव भावनया पञ्च त्वहेयान्यपि न त्रयम् ।।
कामेष्वादौ विपाकौ द्वे लभ्येते नोपपादुकैः ।
तैःषड् वा सप्त वाष्टौ वा षड् रुपेष्वेकमुत्तरे ।।
निरोधयत्युपरमन्नारुप्ये जीवितं मनः ।
उपेक्षां चैव रुपेऽष्टौ कामे दश नवाष्ट वा ।।
क्रममृत्योस्तु चत्वारि शुमे सर्वत्र पञ्च च ।
नवाप्तिरन्त्यफलयोः सप्ताष्टनवभिर्द्वयोः।।[४]

Citta : In the *Yogācāra / Vijñānavāda* system of philosophy

---

4. *Abhidharmakoṣa,* 2. 12-16, ed, Dwarkadass Shastri, Varanasi, 1987, pp.160-168.
(i) See also *Sphutārthavyākhyā* on *Abhidharmakoṣa* 2.12 16, pp. 161– 170. for *rūpadhātu* and *kāmadhātu,*
(ii) Also see for *rūpadhātu and kāmadhātu, Arthaviniścayasūtra,* ed. Samtani, N.H. Patna, 1971, pp.92 and 173.
(iii) All see for *kāmadhātu, Abhidharmadīpa Jaini, P.S. Patna, 1977, pp.17, 84, 91, 139, 146, 245, 302, 343, 363, 374 and 406.*
(iv) Cf. also for *arūpadhātu, Abhidharmakoṣa,* 3.3, p.383:
आरुप्यधातुरस्थानः उपपत्या चतुर्विधः ।
Cf. *Sphutārathabhāṣya on it*: Ibid. p.383,
न ह्यरूपिणां धर्मणां स्थानमस्ति । अतीतानागाविज्ञप्त्यरूपिणो हि धर्मा अदेशस्था इति नियमः।
(v) Cf. Guenther, *Philosophy and Psychology* in the *Abhidharma,* Delhi, 1974, pp.126-127.
(In this world of our experience there are things and events which do not fit the discursive mode of linguistic expression which involves space and time, and which nevertheless are factors to be taken into account).
For a detailed study of *arūpya,* see Guenther, Ibid. pp.126-134.

three terms viz., *citta, manas, vijñāna* and *vijñāpti* are used as synonyms. The Buddhist philosophers believe *cittā* (mind) to be the fundamental and ultimate factor and they treat it as a governing *indriya* which predominates over all objects (*dharmas*) including sense organs, their objects and all other *indriyas*. It may be pointed out that what Vasubandhu wants to convey is that in his system of *Yogācāra / Vijñānavāda* the term *'citta'* is always to be understood in colloboration with three *caittasika* (mental states). Here three the *citta* (mind) and *caittasika* (mental states) belonging to the three wolds are all mere representations of consciousness. What is the purpose of using *'mātrā'* alongwith *citta* in the commentary by Vasubandhu ? According to him the term *'mātra* is used here for exclusion of the external objects. Besides the term *'mātra'* used in the commentary another word, *'artha'* is also used. Normally *'artha'* devotes an object existing in the mundane world. Coming to the term *'citta mātram'* it should be noted that from its various usages both in the *Yogācarā* and *Mādhyamika* works it appears to be associated with purely philosophical and theoretical speculation and also with the spiritual and meditative practice. So we should always be careful with regard to its changing context. Janice Dean Willis observes in the regard, "There is perhaps no term more misunderstood and misinterpreted in the whole of Yogācāra scholarship than cittamātra. Viewed as at once making the most characterictic feature of the school's philosophical doctrine and as, in fact, naming its ontological absolute, this term has come to represent for most scholars the very hall mark of the school. Its literal translation as "mind only" is misleading, implying as it does an absolute idealism. Such a translation is especially mistaken with reference to Asaṅga's works, since for him the term lacks this absolute connotation. *Cittamātra*, throughout the early *Yogācāra*, should more properly be rendered as "just thought" or "merely thought" and seen more appropriately as functioning within the realm of discourse concerned primarily with meditative experience, that is, within discourse about spiritual *practice* as opposed to strictly philosophical theory. (The reader will remember that the earliest name of the school, Yogācāra, was intended to emphasize the primary importance of meditative technique as means of gaining an unimpeded view of ultimate reality). *Cittamātra* is undoubtedly one of the most complex and difficult terms to get a handle on, for a number of reasons.

It is an important term in *Mahāyāna* Buddhism as a whole and so occurs in *both Yogācāra* and *Mādhyamika* works. It occurs with *differing* meanings in various of the *Mahāyāna sūtras* which are said to serve as a specific scriptual authorities for the *Yogācāra* school. It is used in different contexts, and with different intent in what I have called the "early" and 'later" *Yogācāra.* And finally, even within the "early" *Yogācāra,* i.e., within the works of Asaṅga and Vasubandhu *cittamātra* (and its companion term *vijñaptimātra*) seems to have had at least three distinct, intentional uses, depending upon whether, those doctors were addressing themselves to (i) technical information concerning the meditative experience per se, that is, to specific meditative contexts and practice; (2) common sense, prescriptive advice for ordinary beings overly attached to materiality (where it may be said to have had "a provisional meaning", making a sort of intermediate stage in terms of general practice); or (3) the philosophical analysis and description of the cause of ordinary beings' suffering. It is here that we find the Yogācāra's important *epistemological* point that in every ordinary cognition, what is cognized is not an accurate portryal of an object existing outside the mind but merely an object like mental image (*vijñaptimātra*) of that; only a "conceptionalized" object, one that is solely the product of constructive imagination.

However, because of the overriding importance of the term *citta mātra,* an attempt must be made to look at its usages at least within the context of some early *Mahāyāna sūtras,* and the commentarial works of the early Yogācāra. In so doings we must remain constantly mindful of the changing contexts for the term, i.e., whether it is found in contexts related more so purely philosophical and theoretical speculation or in those associated primainly with spiritual and meditative practice."[5]

In order to fully understand what is implied by the usage of the *'mātra'* and *'artha'*; it is essential to understand the process of knowing the reality in Buddhist philosophy and more so in the *Yogācāra / Vijñānavāda.* Before going deeper into the process, we should first of all visualize that an *'artha'* i.e., an external object of the empirical world has two different images viz., (i) perceptnal image and (ii) the conceptual image. The perceptual image projects before over eyes the exact

5. Willis, Janice Dean, *On Knowing Reality* pp.24-26.

dimensional picture of the object of the external world. There is another image which is known as the conceptual image. It may be pointed out that practically for all the schools of Buddhist philosophy the conceptual image is of utmost importance as for as the question of knowing the reality is concerned. In the earlier schools of Buddhist philosophy, i.e. the *Sarvāstivādins*, the *Sautrāntikas* were primainly concerned with the perceptual image of the object existing in the mundane world. For the later schools of Buddhist philosophy i.e. *Mādhyamika* and the *Vijñānavāda*, it was the conceptual image which was of prime importance to them. What is the relation between the perceptual and the conceptual image ? Normally it is presumed that there is one-to-one corespondence between the perceptual and the conceptual image. Here in the context the word *'artha'* denotes an external object of the world. In other words we may say that this is truly a realism for the earlier schools of thought of Buddhism but the later schools of thought of Buddhism denied the perceptual image, i.e. the *'artha'* of the external world. Vasubandhu's major stress is only concerned with the conceptual image which is consciousness only.

It is very interesting in this connection to know how the process of perceptual and conceptual image works through consciousness. Both these images come into existence by means of consciousness only. Herbert V. Guenther says, "Since the process of becoming conscious is not merely a reaction process to the object stimuli but is also a most active process, one in which the sensed material is used for perceiving, or what amounts to the same, where meaning accrues to forms, though this dual presentation of sensed forms and given meanings is due only to the limitation of language with its linear successive order of words, while actually seeing, hearing and so on are themselves process of formulation, we are now able to appreciate the statement concerning the simultaniety of sensation and formation."[6] This process is very nicely illustrated in the *Aṭṭhaśālinī*[7] thus : "Each object makes its way (into consciousness) by way of two doors. Thus a visible object simultaneously with stimulating the sensitivity of the eye apppears at the *manas*

6. Guenther, Herbert V., *Philosophy and Psychology* in the *Abbidharma*, p.27.
7. *Aṭṭhaśālinī*, *Cittopadakāṇḍam Padabhājaniyavaṇṇā*, ed. Ram Shankar Tripathi Varavasi, 1989, p.141.

(*manodvāre*) . The meaning is that the visible object is the irremissible condition for the activation of the unconscious (i.e., of the latent image or deposit of former similar experiences). The process in respect of an audible, olfactory, gustatory, and tactile object is exactly the same (as in respect to a visible object). (This process may be illustrated by a similie). Just as a bird flying through the air and alighting on top of a tree touches a branch of the tree and its shadow strikes on the ground, the touching of the branch and the spreading of the shadow on the ground taking place simultaneously, so also the stimulation of the sensitivity of the eye by the visible object and its appearance at the subjective factor (*manas*) by virtue of its ability to activate the (latest image of the object in the) unconscious takes place simultaneously. After that, the image having been selected from the unconscious continuum immediately after the process first described, and having started with attention and ended with judgement as to the visible object, a conscious perception with respect to any aspect among the visible objects as its objects comes into existence." Yuichi Kajiyama observes in connection with the perception of an external object, "When we are perceiving an external object, say a book, or when we are thinking of an idea, we are usually not conscious of the division of that cognition into these elements. The world of cognition appears at first as an unseparable whole, and it is only through our logical reflection that it is divided into the three. This is the view of the *Sautrāntikas*. The *Sarvāstivāda* philosopher, however, does not believe in the reality of the whole. What is real to him is only the three components parts i.e., the instrument of cognition; the object, and consciousness. In the case of visual perception, for example, the eyes, the colour, and consciousness or understanding of what is seen are realities but visual perception as a whole is not. In the case of cognition of an idea the mind is an insutrument, the idea an object, and consciousness as subject are admitted as real, but not the cognition as a whole. In this case we have to note that the mind as an organ is actually the mind at the preceding moment (*manas*) and that consciousness is the mind at present moment (*Vijñāna*)."[8]

8. Kajiyama, Yuichi, Buddhist Thought and Asian Civilisation, Realsim of the Sarvāstivāda school' (Essays in Honour of Herbert V. Guenther on his sixtienth Birthday). ed. Leslie S. Kawamura & Keith Scott. Dharma Publishing, California, 1977, p.115.

Vasubandhu is trying to say here that what is taken to be subjects and objects of knowledge are only transformations or representation of consciousness. Kochumuttom says, "What Vasubandhu is trying to show is not that the universe is 'representation only' but that what are taken to be the objects of experience are 'representation only'. In short *Viṃśatikā* is polemics not against realism, but against the realistic theory of knowledge."[9]

विज्ञप्तिमात्रमेवैतदसदर्थावभासनात् ।

यथा तैमिरिकस्यासत्केशचन्द्रादिदर्शनम् ।। १ ।।

कश्चिदर्थो नास्ति ।

"On account of the appearances of non-existent objects, it is all mere consciousness only, just like hairs, moons etc., (which do not exist in reality) to a man with a cataract (in his eye)."

(Hence) no external object exists."

What follows now is an interesting debate between one school of thought, which believes in the reality of the objects existing in the world and the *Yogācāra/Vijñānavāda* school of thought of Buddhist philosophy. The earlier schools like *Sarvāstivādins* and *Sautrāntikas* had believed in the reality of the external objects existing in the world. As time passed on, the argument in favour of the external objects being the reality was altogether given up in favour of the consciousness (*vijñapti*) being the only reality. This position was basically held up by the *Yogācāra/Vijñānavāda* school, which went to such an extent of visualising some imaginary objects being visible to a man suffering from cataract in his eyes. In such circumstances he sees more than one hair in place of a single hair and many moons in place of one moon. That is, the objects experienced by such a man do not correspond to extra-mental realities. His experience thus suggests that there could be experiences having no one-to-one correspondence with extra mental objects, which makes a case for Vasubandhu's position. Thus finally it had been established by the *Vijñānavada* school of thought that such an object (*artha*) does not exist. It may also be understood that the *Vijñānavāda* school of thought proposes that not only the external objects

---

9. Kochumuttom, op.cit., p.164.

are unreal; but colours like black, blue and yellow are nothing in themselves but mere projections or representations of consciousness (*vijñapti*) only. This discussion is further carried on also in the kārikās 11-15 where an elaborate discussion takes place whether the form (or colour) is contained in an atom or group of atoms. We shall discuss this in greater details when we come to these kārikās.

अत्र चोद्यते –

यदि विज्ञप्तिरनर्था नियमो देशकालयोः ।

सन्तानस्यानियमश्च युक्ता कृत्यक्रिया न च ।। २ ।।

"If the consciousness is without (extra-mental) objects; then there would no regulation with regard to space and time, there would be the non-observation of regulation of the moment series and there would be no determination of actions prompted (by a particular experience)."

As it has already been pointed out earlier in this context that there is a continuous debate between (i) one school of thought, which believes in the reality of the objects existing in the mundane world, and (ii) the *Yogācāra/Vijñānavāda* school of thought, which denies the reality of the external objects existing in the mundane world and rather believes that the external objects are without any reality and are merely mental projections or representation of consciousness (*vijñapti*) only. As the debate progresses in details, the first school of thought puts its firm objections against the arguments of *Yogācāra/Vijñānavāda* school of thought. We can say that Vasubandhu himself presuming the likelihood of the counter arguments being put forth by the opponents, offers the answers to all the arguments of the opponents.

किमुक्तं भवति ? यदि विना रुपाद्यर्थेन रूपादिविज्ञप्तिरूत्पद्यते, न रुपाद्यर्थात्, कस्मात्, क्वचित् देशे उत्पद्यते न सर्वत्र । तत्रैव च देशे कदाचिद उत्पद्यते न सर्वदा । तद्देशकालप्रतिष्ठितानां सर्वेषां सन्तान उत्पद्यते, न केवलमेकस्य, यथा तैमिरिकाणां सन्ताने केशाद्याभासः,नान्येषाम् । कस्माद यत् तैमिरिकैः केशभ्रमरादि दृश्यते, तेन केशादिक्रिया न क्रियते, न च तदन्यैर्न क्रियते, यदन्नपानवस्त्रविषायुधादि स्वप्ने दृश्यते, तेनान्नादिक्रिया न

क्रियते, न च तदन्यैर्न क्रियते, गन्धर्वनगरेणासत्वात् नगरक्रिया न क्रियते, न च तदन्यैर्न क्रियते, तस्माद् अर्थाभावे देशकालनियमः सन्ताननियमः कृत्यक्रिया च न युज्यते ।

"What is being said? If a consciousness of form etc., arises even without the (corresponding) external objects like form etc., not from the form of an object; why the consciousness is not produced everywhere but only at a particular place? This consciousness is produced only at that (very particular) place sometimes and not always. The consciousness occurs in the stream of all present at those places and at all times, not just in the stream of a single person. For example, the impression of hair etc., appears in the stream of the people ridden with cataract, and not (in the stream of others). How is it that hairs, flies etc., are seen only by the people ridden with cataract in their eyes); and no action is performed by hairs, flies etc., (seen by the people ridden with cataract in their eyes); while it is that (that) by others (some) action is not performed. Food, drink, clothes, poison, weapon etc., (seen) in a dream do not function; while it is not that (that) by others (not seen in a dream) action is not performed. The city of Gandharva does not function like a city on account of being non-existent; while it is not that (that) by others (cities) action is not performed. Therefore, the absence of an object, the regulation of space and time, the non observance of the regulation of moment series and functional viability (*kṛtyakriyā*) do not hold good."[10]

In the above lines Vasubandhu is trying to defend his thesis that consciousness is the only reality of the different external objects existing in the world, i.e., there cannot be any corresponding relation between the perceptual and the conceptual image. All the objects of the world are existing in perceptual form but it is only their conceptual image which is considered as consciousness (*vijñapti*) and that is only real. To this thesis, four different objections are raised by the opponents, who hold that the external objects are the true reality. They (opponents) are raising four possible objections

10. Cf. *Kṛtyakriyā* for its English translation, (i) Kochumuttom translates this as fixed ways of their functioning (Thomas A. Kochumuttom, op.cit., p.261); (ii) Kalupahana translates this as 'fruitful activity' (David. J. Kalapahana, Buddhist Philosophy A Historical Analysis, Hawaii, Honululu, 1976, p.142).

with regard to the regulation of :

(i) place

(ii) time

(iii) non-observance of the regulation of momen. series and

(iv) functional viability (*kṛtyakriyā*).

Now let us consider these objections raised by the opponents in details. Normally an experience is determined by the place and time when, the object is given; it is not, however, determined with regard to the individual enjoying it, in the sense that everybody present at that place and time inevitably has that experience. Alongwith it is also presumed that a particular experience always prompts the same sort of actions. All this is so, it is argued, because the same experience corresponds to extra-mental objects. On the contrary, if such correspondence between experience and objects, is desired, then an experience might happen at any place and time, but not necessarily to everybody; again an experience invariably leads to an action in correspondence with the nature of its object, which would not happen if the experience did not correspond with the object.

Non-observance of the regulation of the moment series: Generally it is believed that blueness or yellowness of an object is visible to all people present where the object is placed. If knowledge of blueness or yellowness is not dependent upon the external object and the observer gets the impression of blueness or yellowness in his moment series and that blueness or yellowness should not be visible to all those present there. Just like the appearance to more than one hair in place of one hair is visible only to a man ridden with a cataract in his eye and not to those (i.e., having the normal vision). Similarly in whose stream, i.e., moment series the cause of the impression of blueness or yellowness is present, only such a man should get the blue or yellow form and not others. But the normal practice in the mundane world is that wherever and a. any time when the impression of blueness or yellowness is created, all the persons present over there and at that moment shall have the impression of blue or yellowness in the normal manner. If the external blueness or yellowness is not there; then there would not be this non-observance of the regulation of the moment series. Here in this particular context the principle of non-observance of the regulation of the moment series means not to be present in the moment series of all but to present specially in the moment series of a fixed or a special type of moment series.

(iv) **Functional viability** (*kṛtyakriyā*): Here the opponents, who hold that external object is real, are raising another very strong objection against the *Yogācāra/Vijñānavādins* by pointing out to the absence of the functional viability (*kṛtyakriyā*). Here the opponents' argument of absence of functional viability (*kṛtyakriyā*) has been further split into three sub-divisions, i.e., (a) false impressions created among the persons ridden with cataract in their eyes (Cf. यथा तैमिरिकाणां सन्ताने...न च तदन्यैर्न क्रियते (b) false impressions of a dream (Cf. यदन्नपानवस्त्रविषायुधादि....न च तदन्यैर्न क्रियते and (c) false impressions regarding the gandharva city etc. (Cf. गन्धर्व नगरेणासत्वात् नगरक्रिया...न च तदन्यैर्न क्रियते)

(a) Among the above mentioned three sub-divisions of the functional viability (*kṛtyakriyā*), we take the first one i.e., false impression created among the persons ridden with cataract in their eyes. In this case, it is presumed that if the knowledge (of an object) is not dependent upon the external object, and the knowledge (consciousness) itself is manifested in the form of an external object; then all the functions or actions (of an object) will be mere manifestations only. In such a situation, the things such as hairs, flies etc., seen by persons ridden with cataract in their eyes, must also function, but this does not happen. Contrary to this all such things as hairs flies etc., seen by the people of clear vision do perform their respective functions.

(b) Even if the external object is not truly real, then in such a situation the things such as food drink, clothes, poison and weapons seen in a dream should perform their respective functions; but this really does not happen. Contrary to this, all such things in the waking stage do perform their respective functions.

(c) Even if the external object is not truly real, then the Gandharva city (city created by a magician in the sky) should be able to perform its normal functions; but this really does not happen. Contrary to this, all cities different from the Gandharva city perform their respective functions.

From all the three examples it is quite clear that from the three false impressions mentioned above in the three different cases no functional viability (*kṛtyakriyā*) is possible (i.e., the things seen in different cases do not perform their functions); similarly in the waking stages also these things fail to perform any viable actions (when the external object is not accepted as truly real).

Thus concluding their arguments against the *Yogācāra/Vijñānavādins*, the opponents, who hold the view that the external object is real, again argue that when the external objects are not accepted as truly real (i) regulation of place, (ii) regulation of time, (iii) non-observance of the regulation of the moment series and (iv) functional viability (*kṛtyakriyā*) would not be possible. And they (opponents) argue that the *Yogācāra/Vijñānavādins* must accept the external object as truly real.

न खलु युज्यते । यस्मात्, देशादिनियमः सिद्धः स्वप्नवत् स्वप्न इव स्वप्नवत् । कथं तावत्, स्वप्ने विनाऽर्थेन क्वचिदेव देशे किञ्चिद् नगरारामस्त्रीपुरुषादिकं दृश्यते, न सर्वत्र । तत्रैव च देशे कदाचिद् दृश्यते, न सर्वकालमिति सिद्धो विनाऽर्थेन देशकालनियमः ।

"No, the objection does not hold good because, the regulation of place and time etc., is established as in a dream. (The term *svapna eva)* like a dream means as if in a dream. How is it (that) in a dream without (corresponding external) objects, the things like city, garden, ladies and men are seen, (and they are seen) not everywhere. They are seen at (that very) place sometimes only (so even without the (external) objects the regulations of place and time, not being universalised are established."

In the above lines, the author of *Vijñaptimātratāsiddhi* tries to meet the objections raised by the believers in the external object's reality. Vasubandhu observes that the dream of certain objects occur only at certain places, and that too, at certain times. Thus, the dream experience too, even though it does not correspond to extra mental objects, is determined by space and time. When in dream a city is seen at a particular place, then this is seen only in a fixed duration of time only. It is not that the city is seen at all times. This only proves that though in a dream there is no external object, the regulations of place and time are to be observed there also.

प्रेतवत् पुनः ।

सन्तानानियमः सिद्ध इति वर्तते । प्रेतानामिव प्रेतवत् । कथं सिद्धं समम् ?

सर्वैः पूयनद्यादिदर्शने ।। ३ ।।

पूयपूर्णा नदी पूयनदी, घृटघटवत्, तुल्यकर्मविपाकावस्था हि प्रेताः सर्वेऽपि पूयपूर्णा नदीं पश्यन्ति,नैक एव । यथा पूयपूर्णाम् एवं मूत्रपुरीषादिपूर्णाम्, दण्डासिधरैश्च, पुरुषैरधिष्ठिताम् इति 'आदि' गृहणेन । एवं सन्तानानियमो विज्ञप्तिनाम् असत्यप्यर्थे सिद्धः ।

"Again as in the case of (the experience) of the ghosts, the non-observance of the regulation of the moment series stands proved. The term "*pretavat*" means like the ghosts. How is the analogy proved? (This analogy) is proved by the sight of pus river etc., by all of them. Pus river means a river full of pus just as *ghṛta-ghaṭa* means a jug full of ghee. The ghosts, who have the similar matured seeds - all of them see the pus river, and not one of them (sees the pus river). Just as the river full of pus, there are also the rivers full of urine, excrement etc., and the places inhabited by the people weilding spears and swords - by the inclusion of the word "*adi*" is meant this. Thus, the non-observance of the regulation of the moment series of the consciousness, even if there are no (corresponding external) objects existing, is proved."

Here in the present context Vasubandhu brings in the examples of the ghosts in order to prove the non-observance of the regulation of the moment series of consciousness even if there being no corresponding external objects. Accordingly the non-observance of the regulation of the moment series (*santānaniyama*) of consciousness is proved in respect of the experience of other beings. It is normally believed that all the ghosts go the hell after the maturity of their deeds (done in this world). Vasubandhu suggests that all the ghosts, when they go to the hell, visualise a river full of pus, even though the fact being that there is not even a drop of pus, what to talk of a river of pus etc., but on account of their own bad deeds they have the projection of a river full of pus and they visualise many other problems connected with such a situation. This projection of the river full of pus is visualised by everybody present in the hell. Not only that, Vasubandhu explains further that these ghosts see also urine and excrement etc., in the river full of pus. It is also that not any one sees them but all of them see them alike. Vasubandhu says that some of the ghosts even see persons wielding swords and lances protecting the river of pus. All the objects are seen by all the ghosts in the hell i.e., at that time and at that place all the ghosts situated in the hell see all these objects. Thus Vasubandhu concluding his arguments in favour of non-observance of the regulation of the moment series of the consciousness says that this is proved even if no external objects corresponding to the river etc., being present over there. The author of *Viṃśatikā* has thus refuted all the four major objections e.g., (i) regulation of place, (ii) regulation of time, (iii) non-observance of the regulation of the moment series (*santānaniyama*) and (iv) functional viability (*kṛtyakriyā*) put by the opponents, who believe in the reality of the external of the world.

नरकवत् पुनः ।

सर्वम् सिद्धमिति वेदितव्यम् । नरकेष्विव नरकवत् । कथं सिद्धम् ?

नरकपालादिदर्शने तैश्च बाधने ।। ४ ।।

यथा हि नरकेषु नारकाणां नरकपालादिदर्शने देशकाल नियमेन सिद्धम्, श्ववायसायसपर्वताद्यागमनगमनदर्शनं वेति 'आदि' ग्रहणेन, सर्वेषां च नैकस्यैव, तैश्च तद्बाधनं सिद्धम्, असत्स्वपि नरकपालादिषु समानस्वकर्मविपाकाधिपत्यात्, ऽन्यत्रापि सर्वमेतद् देशकालनियमादि चतुष्टयं सिद्धमिति वेदितव्यम् ।

"(All the previously mentioned four factors) - as in the case of hell (again). The term *'siddham'* should be interpreted as known. *'Narakavat'* means as if the hells (*'nārakeṣu iva'*). How the four factors are proved? There in the sight of the infernal guards etc., and in the torments by them (all the above mentioned four factors are proved). Just as in the hell the sight of the infernal guards, experienced by the hell-inhabitants proves the regulation of place and time etc., includes similar sights of dogs, birds and coming and going of the iron-mountains. They are seen by all and not merely by one. The torments (being inflicted) upon the hell-inhabitants by the infernal guards are proved. Even though there being no infernal guards etc., all these experiences by the inhabitants of the hells are proved owing to their own matured (seeds of) deeds of the same kind. Thus at other places also all these four: (i) regulation of place, (ii) regulation of time, (iii) non-observance of the regulation of the moment series and

(iv) functional viability (*kṛtyakriyā*) should be known as proved."

It should be understood that uptil now different examples were being given by Vasubandhu in order to meet the various objections raised by his opponents (i.e., *Sautrāntikas* and the *Vaibhāṣikas*), but now an effort is being made collectively to meet all the four objections by one example of the hell. Just as in the case of the hell these four: (i) regulation of place, (ii) regulation of time, (iii) non-observance of the regulation of the moment series and (iv) functional viability (*kṛtyakriyā*) are proved, similarly in the case of the wordly behaviour also the above mentioned four factors are proved to be true even though there being no external objects present corresponding to them. To prove this point, the allied implications of the four cases are to be considered in details in the following lines.

First of all in the case of the hell one has to imagine the two categories of people in the hell; (i) the infernal guards, who happen to be there and (ii) the human beings (*nāraka* or *preta*) who go the hell on the maturity of their bad deeds done in the previous births. In such a situation, when the human beings go the hell, they not only see or visualise the presence of the infernal guards, but they also happen to see big iron made frying pans and other weapons by which the infernal guards appear to torment the hell inhabitants (i.e., human beings who go there after death). By this i.e., the external infernal guards not being there, the regulation of place is proved. Similarly these things are visible to all the inhabitants of the hell present over there only at that very particular time, and not always-this also proves the regulation of time because of external objects not being present over there. In the commentary Vasubandhu has used the word *'adi'* (etc.,). By this word *'adi'* (etc.,) are also meant such things viz., dogs, birds, iron-made mountains and their coming and going. Vasubandhu here means to say that the hell inhabitants also visualise these objects there in the hell. Now, it should be noted in the present context that the above mentioned objects like dogs etc., are projections in the moment series of the beings present over there, it is not that they appear there in anybody's special case only. This basically proves the non-observance of the regulation of the moment series. The allied implications of the four above discussed cases can be summarised as below:

(i) the infernal guards are only imaginary beings, however,

(ii) their experience by the inhabitants of the hell is spatially and temporally restricted to hell,

(iii) this experience is shared by all the inhabitants, and therefore, is not determined with regard to individuals and

(iv) this experience also produces fixed results, viz., torments. Thus the experience in hell refutes all the objections raised by Vasubandhu's opponents who believe in the reality of the external objects.

कि पुनः कारणं नरकपालास्ते च श्वानो वायसा सत्वा नेष्यन्ते ? अयोगात्। न हि ते नारका युज्यन्ते, तथैव तद् दुःखाप्रतिसंवेदनात्। परस्परं यातयताम् 'इमे नारकाः इमे नरकापालाः' इति व्यवस्था न स्यात्। तुल्याकृतिप्रमाणबलानां च परस्परं यातयतां न तथा भयं स्यात्। दाहदुःखं च प्रदीप्तायाम् अयोमय्यां भूमावसहमानाः, कथं तत्र परान् यातयेयुः। अनारकाणां वा नरके कुतः सम्भवः ?

"Again, what is the reason that beings like the infernal guards, dogs and birds are not treated as existent? Because this is inappropriate. They (infernal guards, dogs and birds) cannot be treated as some of the hell-inhabitants (who are condemned to hell); (because) on account of not experiencing the sufferings of hell in a similar way. Tormenting each other, 'These are hell-inhabitants; these are the infernal guards - this arrangement will not be (possible). Being of equal forms (or appearance), measures and strength, how could there be any fear (among them) tormenting each other. Being unable to bear the heat of the flaming iron-like ground; how there (they) could torment others? How can be any possibility of the non-hell beings there in the hells?"

In the present context Vasubandhu alludes to the views of the *Vaibhāṣikas* who hold that dogs and birds etc., present in the hell are human beings. They do not accept them to be the mental projections. According to them all these infernal guards etc., do not have any entity as human beings outside the scope of consciousness. Therefore, they raise here a question as to why infernal guards, the dogs and birds situated in the hells should not be treated as human being. They argue that these are definitely human beings because in appearance they look like human beings.[11]

They make gestures like other human beings and also talk like them. From their bodily gestures and other actions, it can be inferred that they have also a stream of consciousness. If the appearance of the infernal guards etc., is imaginary, then the other human beings may be also proved to be imaginary. To this objection raised by the *Vaibhāṣikas* Vasubandhu says that the infernal guards, dogs and birds etc., cannot be the human beings and he explains his view point in details which are given below. Assuming as if they are human beings of the hell, then they should also feel the torments of the hell like others (like *preta* etc., who are condemned to hell). They do not feel the pain of the torments .ne hell but on the other hand it is they who inflict injuries on others, i.e., when they torture others, they themselves never feel those tortures. And there is none in the hell to torture the infernal guards. Moreover, the bodily gestures and speech etc., which appear in the infernal guards to the hell inhabitants, they do not appear on account of their (infernal guards) stream of consciousness, but they appear to the hell inhabitants on account of the maturity of their own bad deeds performed in the previous births. Normally we get frightened on seeing a ferocious animal like lion etc., painted in a picture and we feel as if they are pouncing upon us, they appear to us to be live but this does not happen because they do not have any stream of consciousness of their own. Here the *Vaibhāṣikas* further argue that the hell inhabitants torture each others. Thus the infernal guards (i.e., tormentors) are the beings of the hell, and those, who are being tormented, are also the beings of the hell; but among them the tormentors are termed as infernal guards (*narakapālas*). To this Vasubandhu replies that those, who are tormenting each other, among them such a situation cannot be imagined in which 'these beings are the infernal guards and those are

---

11. Cf. For infernal guards, dogs, *Bodhicaryāvatāra*, 10.11, ed. Dwarkadass Shastri, Varanasi, 1988, p.427:
त्रैस्ताः पश्यन्त्वकस्मादिह यमपुरुषाः काकगृध्राश्वघोराः ।
ध्वान्तः ध्वस्तं समन्तात् सुखरतिजननी कस्य सौम्या प्रभेयम् ।।

inhabitants of the hell' - because those, who are the infernal guards-, are full of misery and those inhabitants are also full of misery; thus there being no difference in the feeling of pain among both of them. In such a situation a question arises as to who should be called the infernal guards and who should be designated as the hell inhabitants. Moreover, if the infernal guards are also the hell inhabitants like others, then both i.e., the infernal guards and the hell inhabitants will be of same form, measure and of equal strength. It is usually said about the hell that those sinners, who are condemned to hell, when they see before them very powerful ferocious and fearful guards, become very terrified and start trembling on their sight. In such a situation they even try to run away from there but on finding complete darkness they are unable to run from there. In order to prove that the condemned sinners of the hell and the infernal guards both belong to the two distinct category, Vasubandhu says that if both of them feel the torments of the hell alike; then how these infernal guards will be able to inflict such torments on the sinners, when they themselves are feeling the agony of the torments. When they (the infernal guards) themselves cannot stand on the earth burning with heat; how they (infernal guards) can torment others (i.e., hell inhabitants - the sinners). In the face of these difficulties Vasubandhu argues that the so called infernal. guards are mere psychological projections of the consciousness of the hell inhabitants.

कथं तावत् तिरश्चां स्वर्गसंभव ? एवं नरकेषु
तिर्यक्प्रेतजिशेषाणां नरकपालादीनां सम्भवः स्यात् ।

"How indeed are the animals born in heaven? The animals, ghosts, infernal guards etc., are also born in the hell in the same manner."

In the present controversy as to what is the relation between the infernal guards and the condemned sinners of the hell the *Vaibhāṣikas* are raising a point. How it is possible that the animals can take birth in the hell besides the infernal guards and the condemned sinners. They (*Vaibhāṣikas*) are asking how the non-hell beings can be born in the hell. To them Vasubandhu puts a counter question: how are the animals born in the heaven? People say that in the heaven besides the gods there are many things viz., the *Airāvata* elephant, goose, swam and parrots etc. Vasubandhu says that if the animals can possibly be found (or can take birth) in the heaven; how they cannot be similarly in the heaven; how they cannot similarly be born in the hell. Thus the presence of dogs, birds and other animals is fully justified in the hell besides the infernal guards and the hell habitants.

तिरश्चां सम्भवः स्वर्गे यथा न नरके तथा ।

न प्रेतानां यतस्तज्जं दुःखं नानुभवन्ति ते ।। ५ ।।

ये हि तिर्यञ्चः स्वर्गे सम्भवन्ति, ते तद्भाजनलोकसुखसंवर्तनीयेन कर्मणा तत्र सम्भूताः तज्जं सुखं प्रत्यनुभवन्ति, न चैवं नरकपालादयो नारकं दुःखं प्रत्यनुभवन्ति, तस्मात् न तिरश्चां सम्भवो युक्तो प्रेतानाम् ।

"Animals are born in the heaven; they are not born in the hell in a similar way. The infernal guards are not born in the hell (because) they do not experience the myseries of hell. The animals, who are born in the heaven, enjoy the pleasure accruing from the deeds due to which they are born there. They are the enjoyers of the pleasure of that region. The infernal guards do not experience the infernal feelings. Therefore, neither the birth of animals nor of infernal guards (in the hell) is appropriate."

Here Vasubandhu intends to make a distinction between the people, who go to the heaven on account of their good deeds on the one side and the sinners condemned to he hell on other side. This distinction can be understood in the following way. Normally the position is like this that beings of a particular region experience the pleasures and pains of that region, e.g., when a citizen of a country goes to another country; then he not only fully enjoys the pleasures of social and cultural activities of that country but he is bound to enjoy the beauties of pleasure-groves, garden rivers, mountains and the seasons of that country along with the pleasures and the pains associated with them. Accordingly the animals are born in the heaven provided they deserve this by their good deeds. However, the infernal guards do not deserve the hell, through their deeds, for in that case they would be both in the same boat as those condemned to hell, and, therefore, would not be tormentors. Now, the opponents want to suggest that they are what the hell inhabitants by virtue of their deeds project them. This suggestion, too, does not satisfy Vasubandhu.

तेषां तर्हि नाराकणां कर्मभिस्तत्र भूतविशेषाः भवन्ति वर्णाकृतिप्रमाणबलविशिष्टाः ये नरकपालादिसंज्ञां प्रतिलभन्ते । तथा च परिणामन्ति यद् विविधां हस्तविक्षेपादिक्रियां कुर्वन्तो दृश्यन्ते भयोत्पादार्थम् , यथा मेषाकृतयः पर्वता आगच्छन्तो गच्छन्तः अयःशाल्मलीवने च कण्टका अधोमुखीभवन्त ऊर्ध्वमुखी भवन्तश्चेति । न ते न सम्भवन्त्येव ।

"Then due to the deeds of the hell inhabitants some special beings are born, who are of special colour, form, measure and strength- these (very special beings) get the nomenclatures of infernal guards etc. They transform themselves so as to appear to perform the movement of hand etc. in order to create fear. They appear in the form of ram-mountain-coming and going; in an iron forest (they appear in the form of) thorns turning up and down. It is not that they are nor born at all."

In the above context Vasubandhu is stating the opponent's (i.e., *Sautrāntika*) point of view saying that according to them all these hell inhabitants etc., condemned to hell are *Mahābhūtas* and are born on account of their deeds. But this view is not acceptable to Vasubandhu who holds that they are transformations of the hell inhabitants.

यदि तत्कर्मभिस्तत्र भूतानां सम्भवस्तदा ।
इष्यते परिणामश्च किं विज्ञानस्य नेष्यते ।। ६ ।।

विज्ञानस्यैव तत्कर्मभिस्तथा परिणामः कस्मान्नेष्यते, किं पुनर्भूतानि कल्पन्ते ।

"If the (special) beings can be born from their (i.e., hell inhabitants) deeds and they are supposed to be the transformations, then why not recognise them as transformations of their consciousness?

Why not they are recognised (as) the transformations of consciousness issuing from their deeds? Why are they imagined as special beings?"

Here Vasubandhu is presenting a difficulty faced by the *Sautrāntikas* who say that the object associated with the consciousness of the hell inhabitants (objects like burning earth, iron-mountain etc.,) are the true realities outside the realm of consciousness. They are produced out of the deeds of the hell inhabitants just as in the human world the consciousness of mountain trees etc., are produced, but they are not produced without the external real objects. Therefore, according to the *Sautrāntikas* the mountain and trees etc., are the real objects. Vasubandhu finds an additional difficulty in accepting that the infernal guards could be projections of one's own deeds; viz., that such a situation implies that the deeds do not produce their fruits in the same place where they were done.

अपि च

कर्मणो वासनाऽन्यत्र फलमन्यत्र कल्प्यते ।

तत्रैव नेष्यते यत्र वासना किं नु कारणम् ।। ७ ।।

येन हि कर्मणा नारकाणां तत्र तादृशो भूतानां सम्भवः कल्प्यते परिणामश्च, कर्मणो वासना तेषां विज्ञानसन्तानसन्निविष्टा, नान्यत्र । यत्रैव वासना, तत्रैव तस्याः फलं तादृशो विज्ञान परिणामः किं नेष्यते । यत्र वासना नास्ति तत्र तस्याः फलं कल्प्यते । इति किमत्र कारणम् ।

"The impression of a deed is imagined somewhere else; and its fruit is imagined elsewhere. Why not recognise the fruit where there is the impression?

That type of birth of special beings and their transformations is imagined due to the deeds of hell inhabitants. The impression of their deeds is penetrated into their stream of consciousness, and nowhere else: why not recognise that where there is the impression there itself is the fruit in form of transformation? Where there is the no impression, there its fruit is not imagined. What is the reason?"

In the 7th *kārikā* Vasubandhu is raising certain objections to a theory according to which the impressions generate certain fruits-no matter the impressions might exist some where else and the fruit thereof might be some where else. In other words this was the position taken by the *Sautrāntikas* who are raising these objections against Vasubandhu. Here the whole discussion centres one important poiont, i.e., as to what is the position of the *Mahābhūtas* which appear to the hell inhabitants in the hell. According to the *Sautrāntikas* these *Mahābhūtas* appear independently and are not born out of the deeds of the hell inhabitants. But the position of the *Vijñānavādins* is different and they say that the impression of the deeds are embeded in the stream of consciousness; therefore, the infernal guards and all their actions (like anger and tormenting the hell inhabitants) should be placed in the stream of consciousness and not among the *Mahābhūtas*; because at a point of time when there were the deeds of the hell-inhabitants, the *Mahābhūtas* were not there. Thus when and where in the stream of consciousness that matured impression of the deed is present, at that very moment and in that very stream the afore-said consciousness should appear in the transformations in the form of impressions. But this position is not acceptable to the *Sautrānikas* who take these *Mahābhūtas* as external objects where there is no impression, they accept them there to be fruit of their actions. In brief it appears that Vasubandhu is asking the *Sautrāntikas* that what is the reason of saying : where there is no impression, why its fruit is imagined there. In the other words the position could be stated like this that in nowhere in the world the seeds put in a field could generate its fruit on the mountain.

आगमः कारणम् । यदि विज्ञानमेव रूपादिप्रतिभासं स्यात्, न रूपादिकोऽर्थः, तदा रूपाद्यायतनास्तित्वं भगवता नोक्तं स्यात् ।

"The scripture is the reason. If the consciousness were to appear as form, colour etc., and not the object contained in the form and colour, then the existence of the (of knowledge) form etc., would not have been stated by the Lord."

In the present and the following lines Vasubandhu is interpreting the theory of bases of knowledge (*āyatanas)* in his own way. As a matter of fact, Vasubandhu is trying to counter examine the theory of the *Sautrāntikas*, whose point of view is put forth in the above lines. The *Sautrāntikas* are said to be real followers of saying of the Lord (Cf. ये सूत्रप्रमाणिका न शास्त्राप्रमाणिका ते सौत्रान्तिकाः) । The Lord Buddha is said to have propounded that there are twelve bases of knowledge; (i) *cakṣurāyatana,* (ii) *śrotrāyatana* (iii) *ghrāṇāyatana,* (iv) *jivhyātana,* (v) *kāyātana,* (vi) *manāyatana,* (vii) *rūpāyatana,* (viii) *ṣabdāyatana,* (ix) *gandhāyatana,* (x) *rasāyatana,* (xi) *spraṣṭavyāyatana* and (xii) *dharmāyatana*. According to the *Sautrātantikas* point of view, if the consciousness only were to appear in the form of colour etc., then there would not have been anything present there other than the consciousness; and moreover, why the twelve bases of knowledge would have been enumerated in the works like the *Abhidharmakoṣa* etc. In the present situation i.e., in the hell the *Mahābhūtas* appear to the hell- inhabitants as a distinct entity other than the eye-consciousness of them. It means that these *Mahābhūtas* are there in the hell on account of their decisive factor (*adhipatiphala*) of the hell inhabitants and they are not there on account of their maturity of deeds. The maturity of the deeds is only where there is the seed of the actions. This is not applicable in the case of decisive factor (*adhipatiphala*). They may appear in a different place other than that of their seeds. To these views of the opponents i.e., *Sautrāntikas* Vasubandhu replies that the Buddha's statement that there are the twelve bases of knowledge (*āyatanas*), has to be understood in such a way that as knowable objects (*spraṣṭvya* etc.,) and the senses (*cakṣus* etc.,) they are transformations or representations of consciousness, i.e., bases of knowledge (*āyatanas* are the externalisation of the seeds of the subjectivity (represented by the sense organs) and objectivity (represented by the so called objects). According to him, by the bases of knowledge (*āyatanas*), the Buddha meant such transformations of consciousness.

अकारणमेतद् ।

यस्मात् रूपाद्यायतानास्तित्वं तद् विनेयजनं प्रति ।

अभिप्रायवशादुक्तमुपपादुकसत्ववंत् ।। ८ ।।

यथा 'अस्ति सत्व उपपादुकः' इत्युक्तं भगवता अभिप्रायवशाच्चित्तसन्तत्यनुच्छेदमायत्यामभिप्रेत्य । "नास्ति सत्व आत्मा वा धर्मास्त्वेते सहेतुकाः" इति वचनात् । एवं रुपाद्यतनास्तित्वमप्युक्तं भगवता तद्देशनाविनेयजनमधिकृत्याभिप्रायिकं तद्वचनम् ।

"This is not the reason, because the existence of the bases of knowledge (such as colour etc.,) was preached by (the Lord) for the humble people (disciples) with a hidden meaning; just like the being born by metamorphosis was stated by him.

Just as 'there are beings (apparently) born by metamorphosis' - this has been stated by the Lord as a hidden meaning keeping in view the unbroken stream of mind.

"There is no being-atman or dharmas - all these are (caused) with conditions" - this is confirmed by this saying (of the Lord). In the same manner the existence of the bases of knowledge (such as colour etc.,) has been preached by the Lord for the humble people (disciples) with a hidden meaning (this saying is to be treated like a hidden meaning)."

Uptil now the *Sautrāntikas* have been trying their best to

prove the reality of the external objects of the empirical world. Vasubandhu challenges them by saying that quoting the scriptures in this connection does not carry any weight. They (opponents) had said that the Lord Buddha had himself spoken about the twelve bases of knowledge (*āyatanas* quoted earlier) in his early discourses to his pupils. Thus according to the *Sautrāntikas* the form could be contained in these twelve bases of knowledge (*āyatanas*). Vasubandhu states that these twelve bases of knowledge (*āyatanas*) were preached by the Lord keeping in view the mental acumen of the disciples with a hidden meaning (*abhiprāyavaśāt*). It must be understood that the teachings of the Lord are of two categories; (i) direct meaning (*nītārtha* = *pārmārthika*) and (ii) hidden meaning or an expedient meaning (*neyārtha* = *vyavahārika*). The former preaching i.e., (*nītārtha*) is meant for the higher class of people (*āryajana*) while the latter type of teaching (*neyārtha*) is meant for the common masses (*pṛthakjana*).[12]

In the present context the second type of preaching i.e., hidden meaning (*neyārtha*) has been referred to here as '*abhiprāyavaśāt*'. Lord Buddha realising that the ordinary people cannot fully comprehend the higher concepts like the non-substantiality of *dharma* and *ātman* (*dharmanairātmya* and *pudgalanairātmya*), he initially preached twelve bases of knowledge (*āyatanas*). This type of the discourse or preaching was liked by the ordinary people and Buddha had realised that they would be gradually matured enough in future and subsequently will be able to fully understand the significance of the higher concepts like the non-substantiality of *dharma* and *ātman* (*dharmanairātmya* and *pudgalanairātmya*) and he had known that if the ordinary people were initiated to these two concepts, then owing to their feeble mind they might misinterpret them. Thus realising this situation by his skillful means (*upāyakauśala*) he preached the reality of the external *dharmas*. As the Lord had preached the bases of knowledge (*āyatanas*), similarly he had also preached the being born by

12. Cf. Candrakīrti's *Prasannapadā* on *Madhyamakaśāstra* 15.11. p.119:
(i) तथाविधविनेयजनबोधानुरोधात् तु परमार्थदर्शनस्य उपायभूतत्वात् नेयार्थत्वेन भगवता महाकरुणापरतन्त्रतया विज्ञानादिवादो देशितः साम्मितीय पुदगलवादवत् न नीतार्थं इति विज्ञेयम् ।
(ii) Cf. *Sandhinirmocanasūtra* 7.5 (Quoted in Candrakīrti's *Prasannapadā*, op.cit. p.120:
नीतार्थसूत्रान्तविशेष जानति यथोपदिष्टा सुगतेन शून्यता ।
यस्मिन् पुनः पुद्गल सत्व पूरुषो नेयार्थतो जानति सर्वधर्मान् ।।

metamorphosis. It may be said that in the early Buddhism there was a great deal of discussion about the life or consciousness being present after death or not. As a matter of fact this question was even posed to Buddha in a different context but he maintained his silence in reply to this question along with other fourteen irrelevant questions. To quote Kalupahana in this connection, "The statement that the tathāgata gives up the five aggregrates after death and that these aggregates are completely destroyed does not mean that he exists in a different form, nor that he is completely annihilated. Just as it is impossible to know whether the tathāgata or the arhat survives death, even so, it is not possible to know whether he is annihilated after death. if, after dying that the tathāgata survives death, the Buddha had maintained that he is annihilated, he would have been guilty of saying something that is not based or dependent on any source of knowledge. Hence, the most reasonable way to interpret the Buddha's statement on this problem and not misinterpret him would be to say that the state of the arhat after death cannot be known by the available means of knowing (pramāṇa). This explains the Buddha's decision to leave these questions undeclared (*avyākṛta*). It is in this light only that we should interpret the Buddha's answer to the question raised in the *Suttanipāta* (1076) : "is the one who had achieved the goal annihilated or he is eternally free from illness"? [13] It must be admitted that these are some of the very difficult questions to be answered and any attempt to find out a suitable answer to these questions would be a futile exercise. Kalupahana says, "And it may be observed here that the Buddha himself, for a variety of reasons, refused to answer has been the bane of Buddhist scholarship, classical as well as modern".[14]

We have explained above as to why the Lord Buddha had preached the twelve bases of knowledge (*āyatanas*) for the ordinary people. Now the question arises: why Buddha has also spoken about the beings born by metamorphosis (*upapaduka sattva*) ? In order to know the implications of this question we have to refer to two important concepts, i.e., annihilism (*uccedavāda*) and eternalism (*śāśvatavāda*), which were quite prevalent on the Indian philosophical scene when

13. Kalupahana, David, J., Buddhist Philosophy, A Historical Analysis, Honululu, 1976, p.80.
14. Ibid. p.85.

Buddhism started formulating its own ideas in a proper perspective. According to the first view the people in general had thought that there was no life process in their earlier lives and this would not be even in their future lives. Thus they were of the firm belief that there was no past life and there would not be any future life (process). In such a situation it was supposed that these people would be wanton people without caring for the *kuśala karman* (good action) and *akuśala* action (bad action). In order to satify such a class of people and with the intention that these people might follow the righteous course, the Lord Buddha spoke to them about the beings born by metamorphosis (*upapāduka* sattva). The *upapāduka sattva* is a class of beings[15] in which there is no change and for their birth, there is no need of father and mother. These beings are born accidently without any cause. It must be noted that some of the people liked the idea of human beings also coming into existence without any previous life process. They did not like the idea that the life-process was prevalent in the earlier birth and this would continue in the next birth also. Buddha had known the liking of the common masses for the non-continuity of the life process in the past and future births. He accordingly spoke to them about the beings born by metamorphosis (*upapāduka sattva*). This shows that Buddha had devised a novel idea of preaching about the beings born by metamorphosis (*upapāduka sattva*). This was greatly liked by his pupils (*vineyajana*), who firmly believed in annihilism (*ucchedavāda*). By this preaching these people knew that the lord was talking about a life process which did not exist in the past life and would not take place even in the next birth.

कोऽत्राभिप्रायः ?

यतः स्वबीजाद विज्ञप्तिर्यदाभासा प्रवर्तते ।
द्विविधायतनत्वेन ते तस्या मुनिरब्रवीत ।। ९ ।।

---

15. Cf. *Abhidharmakośa*, 3. 8-9, pp.401-402:
चतस्रो योनयस्तत्र सत्वानामण्डजादयः ।
चतुर्धा नरतिर्यञ्चो नारका उपपादुकाः ।
अन्तराभवदेवाश्च प्रेता अपि जरायुजाः ।।
also Cf. *Sphutārtha-bhāṣya* on it, pp.401-402:
सर्वैश्च प्रत्यङ्गैल्यादिभिरुपेताः सकृदुंपजायन्ते न, कललाद्यनुपूर्व्या अण्डजादिवत्,।
उपपादने उपपत्तौ साधुकारित्वात्,। शुक्लशोणिताद्यनुपादानेन न सकृदुपजातत्वात् उपपादुका इत्युच्यन्ते ।।

किमुक्तं भवति ? रूपप्रतिभासा विज्ञप्तियतः स्वबीजात् परिणामविशेषप्राप्ताद् उत्पद्यते, तच्च बीजम्, तत्प्रतिभासा च सा, ते तस्या विज्ञप्तेश्चक्षरूपायतनत्वेन यथाक्रमं भगवानब्रवीत्। एवं तावत् स्प्रष्टव्य प्रतिभासा विज्ञप्तिर्यतः स्वबीजात् परिणामविशेषप्राप्राद् उत्पद्यते , तच्च बीजम्, यत्प्रतिभासा च सा, ते तस्याः कायस्प्रष्टव्यायतनत्वेन यथाक्रमं भगवानब्रवीद् इत्ययमभिप्रायः ।

"What is the hidden meaning?, wherefrom its own seed a representation of consciousness develops, the sage spoke of the two bases of knowledge, the representation in the form in which that consciousness appears.

What is being said? A representation of consciousness appears as form - this arises from its own (namely) of the seed that is the seed, that representation of consciousness is that of the same form. These two i.e., *cakṣurāyatna* and the *rūpāyatana* have been respectively spoken by the Lord as (to have been born out of that) consciousness. In the same manner representation of consciousness appears as an object of touch the consciousness itself arises from its maturity of seed. This seed and the from in which it appears, are respectively what the Lord spoke of as two bases, i.e., body *āyatna* and the touch *āyatna* repectively this is the (hidden) meaning."

Vasubandhu is now explaining the theory of (*āyatana*) bases of knowledge in relation to consciousness and seed. It may be understood thus that when the seed is matured enough, it gives birth to two different *āyatanas,* i.e., (i) *cakṣurāyatana* and (ii) *rūpāyatana*. These two *āyatanas* may also be designated as : (i) *ādhyātmika āyatana* and (ii) *bāhya āyatana*. When the form is manifested in the eye consciousness, the two are important, e.g., *cakṣurvijñāna* and the appearance of the form therein. Both of them are transformations of the same seed. viz., they both are the transformations of the same matured predisposition (*vāsanā*). This may be explained in another way viz., the matured seed externalises itself through the medium of the eye consciousness. This process is repeated in the cases of the other sense organs, e.g., a matured seed of the body may give rise to two *āyatanas,* i.e., (i) *kāyatana* and (ii) *spraṣṭavya āyatana* and this is true of other bases of knowledge also. How a consciousness of an object is produced with the help of two *āyatanas* (bases of knowledge), as stated

in the *kārikā* no.9. This may be understood with help of the diagram:

Diagram

Seed (*Vāsanā*) *Ālayavijnāna*

Eye (Consciousness) (*Cakṣurāyatana*)

From (*Rūpa*) of the object (*Rūpāyatana*)

Both i.e., eye and form (as spoken of the two *āyatanas* in the *kārikā* no.9) when combined together form the consciousness (reality) of the object.

एवं पुनरभिप्रायवशेन देशयित्वा को गुणः ?

तथा पुद्गलनैरात्म्य प्रवेशो हि

तथा हि देश्यमाने पुद्गलनैरात्म्यं प्रविशन्ति । द्वयाद् विज्ञानषट्कं प्रवर्तते, न तु कश्चिद् एको द्रष्टाऽस्ति न यावन्मन्ता- इत्येवं विदित्वा ये पुद्गलनैरात्म्यदेशनाविनेयास्ते पुद्गलनैरात्म्यं प्रविशन्ति ।

"What again is the purpose of (having) instructed of the hidden meaning?

Thus one enters the (domain) of non-substantiality of this self (*pudgala*), being thus instructed the disciples enter into the (domain) of non-substantiality of the self (*pudgala*). By the twins (of subject and object) eightfold consciousness starts, there is no one as a perceiver and nor a thinker the disciples having known thus the non-substantiality of the self (*pudgala*) enter into the (domain) of the non-subatantiality of the self (*pudgala*)."

Vasubandhu has already explained earlier that the *āyatanas* (bases of knowledge) representing subjectivity and objectivity, are the projections of consciousness. The *Sautrāntikas* are questioning the *Vijñānavādins*: what is purpose of instructing about the (*āyatanas*). Is there any hidden meaning in them? As a matter of fact, Vasubandhu is now trying hard to hit those who had believed earlier in the existence of a permanent soul or self loosely designated by the word *pudgala*. The believers in the permanent soul or self had contended that there is an eternal, permanent soul, which is the perceiver of the form, which is the enjoyer of the different objects of this world. It has already been mentioned earlier that Buddha had talked about the twelve bases of knowledge (*āyatanas*). The twelve *āyatanas* may be divided into (i) six internal *āyatanas* and (ii) six external *āyatanas*. As far as the actual process of consciousness (*vijñāna*) taking place is concerned, it has already been explained earlier that the six internal sense organs give rise to the six outer *āyatanas*. There were people who had earlier believed that there was an eternal, permanent and independent entity known as *ātman* (or *pudgala*) independent of the sense organs, which enjoyed different objects of the world. To this Vasubandhu is replying that there is not any perceiver or thinker as such (independent of the six sense organs). Here Vasubandhu suggests that there is no need of accepting any such entity known as *ātman* or *pudgala*,[16] because all such activities of perceiving and thinking are performed by the sense organs as *cakṣurvijñāna* etc., (eye consciousness). Thus having incorporated all activities concerning the sense organs and the object under the twelve *āyatanas*, Vasubandhu declares that there is no existence of any eternal, permanent and independent *ātman* or *pudgala*. This is known as non-substantiality of the self (*pudgalanairātmya*). Thus the ordinary people once having realised the futility of the non-substantiality of the self enter into domain of non-substantiality of the dharma.[17]

अन्यथा पुनः ।

देशना धर्मनैरात्म्यप्रवेशः

'अन्यथा' इति विज्ञप्तिमात्रदेशना । कथं धर्मनैरात्म्यप्रवेशः ? विज्ञप्तिमात्रमिदं रूपादिधर्मप्रतिभासमुत्पद्यते, न तु रूपादिलक्षणो धर्मः कोऽप्यस्तीति विदित्वा ।

"Otherwise again, by this instruction one enters into the (domain) of the non-substantiality of the objects (*dharmas*). (Here) the (term) 'Otherwise' means the mere instruction about representation of consciousness. How one enters into the (domain) of non-substantiality of the objects? Having (once) known that there are no objects like colour etc., as such; (and) that mere representations of consciousness

---

16. For a detailed discussion on pudgala, see *Pudgalaviniścaya, Abhidharmakoṣa*, ed. Dwarkadass Shastri, Varanasi, 1987, pp.1187-1234.
17. For *Pudgalanairātmya* and *Dharmanairātmya*, see, supra pp. 24-28

produce the appearance of the objects like the colour etc. (How one enters into the domain of non-substantiality of the objects?".

The whole discussion reveals that there are certain stages of realisation at different levels of consciousness. First of all, one has to realise the non-substantiality of the self (*pudgala-nairātmya*). Now, the question arises if one can get *Niravāṇa* only by acquiring the knowledge of non-substantiality of the self, then what is the utility of instructing the representation of consciousness ? Is not mere representation of consciousness enough in itself for realizing *Nirvāṇa* ? Here Vasubandhu explains as to what is significance of instructing the representation of consciousness. He asserts that the representation of consciousness leads to the non-substantiality of the objects (*dharmas*). The basic teaching of *Viṃśatikā* is that the consciousness only is reflected into the external (formal) objects having different colours etc. As a matter of fact, there is nothing existing independently in this empirical world except the mind, or consciousness. When one realises this, he enters into the domain of non-substantiality of the objects (*dharmanairātmya*).

यदि तर्हि सर्वथा धर्मो नास्ति, तदपि विज्ञप्तिमात्रं नास्तीति कथं तर्हि व्यवस्थाप्यते ?

न खलु सर्वथा धर्मो नास्तीत्येवं धर्मनैरात्म्यप्रवेशो भवति, अपितु कल्पितात्मना ।। १० ।।

यो बालैर्धर्माणां स्वभावो ग्राह्यग्राहकादि परिकल्पितः तेन कल्पितेनात्मना तेषां नैरात्म्यम्, न त्वनभिलाप्येनात्मना यो बुद्धानां विषय इति ।

"If therefore, there is no object at all, there is not even the representation of consciousness also. (Then) how (the theory of mere representation of consciousness) is established ? The entry into the (domain) of the non-substantiality of the objects does not at all mean that there is no object altogether. But on the contrary (one enters into the domain of non-substantiality of the objects) on account of the (absence of the) imagined nature (or character) of the object. That nature (or character) of the objects as graspable and grasper etc., which is imagined by the ignorant people, the non-substantiality of that imagined nature is (really) the non-substantiality of the objects (of the knowledge) of the enlightened ones."

In the preceding lines it has been established that the non-substantiality of self and object (*pudgala* and *dharma-nairātmya*) applies only to their imagined nature (*kalpitātma*). This is very useful in understanding Vasubandhu's view of reality. When the *Vijñānavādins* had talked about the non-substantiality of the objects (*dharmas*): then it occured to those who believed in the reality of the external objects, that by establishing the non-substantiality of the self, *ātman* or *pudgala* had been proved to be a non-entity. Similarly by this non-substantiality of the objects (*dharmas*) the objects would also prove to be a non-entity. Keeping these views in mind they (believers in the reality of the external objects) are raising these objections to the *Vijñānavādins*. While talking about the non-substantiality of the objects (*pudgalanairātmya*) Vasubandhu speaks of the imagined (*kalpita*) nature of the things. Before going further into other details of the discussion it is useful to understand the three concepts i.e., imagined (*kalpita*), dependent (*paratantra*) and absolute (*pariniṣpanna*). In the Buddhist philosophical system the whole of the phenomena has been divided into *samvṛtti* and absolute (*parmārtha*). Phenomena is further divided into two i.e., the subject (*ātma*) and object (*dharma*). The objects of the world have no nature of their own; they have no reality. They are merely imagined to exist and have no intrinsic existence of their own. They are, therefore, imagined (*kalpita*). To be dependent is the phenomenal aspect of the unreal object. This is known as the *paratantra* because it denotes the subjective. The third is the absolute (*pariniṣpanna=paramārtha*). It is the pure consciousness undefiled by the least trace of the objectivity when dependent (*paratantra*) is purified from the false duality imposed upon it by the imagined (*parikalpita*), it becomes absolute (*pariniṣpanna*).[18] After this Vasubandhu speaks of non-substantiality of the objects (*dharmanairātmya*). It must be pointed out that the word '*dharmanairātmya* is generally misunderstood among the Buddhist philosophical concepts. What is the meaning of this term ? The ignorant people (*pṛthagjana*) think that all the objects of the world possess some functions like the graspable and the grasper. They think that these functions are associated with the very nature (*svabhāva*) of the objects but as a matter of fact, this is not so. The objects in themselves are nothing (*śūnya*) and they

18. See, supra p.24 for *parikalpita*, *parapantra* and *pariniṣpanna*.

are thus unreal. What we do in the world, is to superimpose these unreal functional activities on them whereas they themselves are not at all capable of performing any such activities. Thus accordingly all the functions of the objects are only imagined (*kalpita*) and they are not real. To negate these functional activities of the objects, that is to say, to separate the functional activities from the objects is really the non-substantiality of the objects (*dharmanairātmya*). To the ignorant people it appears that as if the eye consciousness is the grasper and the other qualities associated with the object as colour etc., are externally present apart from the eye-consciousness. The ignorant people presume that there is something other than the consciousness externally real. Thus the external qualities such as blue etc., are only imagined (*kalpita*) and they are not real. As a matter of fact, the absence of these external qualities such as blue etc., is really designated by the term *dharmanairātmya* (non-substantiality of the objects). It must also be understood that by the usage of the term i.e., *dharmanairātmya* the total negation of the worldly objects is not intended. On the contrary, Vasubandhu says that the reality or nature of things is ineffable and only the enlightened ones can realise this. This ineffable nature or aspect of reality, which becomes neither subject nor the object of experience, is the suchness (*tathatā*), the thing as it is, and therefore, substantial. To quote Thomas A. Kochumuttom, "Vasubandhu makes a clear distinction between the imagined aspect of reality (*kalpita*) and ineffable (*anabhilāpya*) aspect of reality. It is the imagined aspect of reality that becomes either subject or object of an ordinary man's experience, while its ineffable aspect is far beyond the range of his experience. Consequently, it is the forms of subjectivity and objectivity that are traced to imagination (*parikalpita* or *vikalpa*), and, therefore, called the transformation of consciousness (*vijñāna pariṇāma*) and characterised as non-substantial (*nairātmya*)."[19]

एवं विज्ञप्तिमात्रास्यापि विज्ञप्त्यन्तरपरिकल्पितेनात्मना नैरात्म्यप्रवेशाद् विज्ञप्तिमात्रव्यवस्थापनया सर्वधर्माणां नैरात्म्यप्रवेशो भवति, न तु तदस्तित्वापवादात् इतरथा हि विज्ञप्तेरपि विज्ञप्त्यन्तरमर्थः स्यादिति विज्ञप्तिमात्रत्वं न सिध्येत, अर्थवतीत्वाद् विज्ञप्तीनाम् ।

19. Kochumuttom Thomas A, A Buddhist Doctrine of Experience, p.173.

"Similarly a representation of consciousness is non-substantial with regard to the nature imagined by another representation of consciousness. In this way one enters the (domain) of non-substantiality of the representation of consciousness and it is through this entry (into the domain of non-substantiality of the object), which establishes the doctrine of mere representation of consciousness, one enters into the theory of non-substantiality of the objects, and not through the denial of their existence. Otherwise if a representation of consciousness would have an object, which will be different from the representation of consciousness; and thus the representation of consciousness having an object, this theory consciousness will not be proved at all."

We have already pointed out earlier that the objects are present in the empirical world from the *saṃvṛtti* point of view. No school of Buddhist philosophy denies the existence of things in the world. The whole discussion is based on the very existence of the things of the world irrespective of the position any school of thought of Buddhist philosophy may hold. In this context Vasubandhu is pointing out to a major difficulty of visualising such a situation in which one representation of consciousness may require another representation of consciousness, which would again require an object (which is bound to have imagined nature according to the theory of consciousness). We have earlier seen that the objects have no fixed nature of their own. We have falsely imposed the functional activities on them. The second representation of consciousness cannot have any object for it because the whole discussion is not based on the denial of the basic existence of the things (*dharmas*). If this process is allowed to continue, then one representation of consciousness would require another representation of consciousness having an object qualifying with it. This would imply that every representation of consciousness would possess a qualifying object associated with it. If this is so, every representation of consciousness will entail another representation of consciousness and ultimately it may lead to *infinite regress*. This will mean that the claim of the *Vijñānavādins* to prove only consciousness to be the reality would be untrue. It will be a rather difficult task to prove the theory of consciousness being the reality.

कथं पुनरिदं प्रत्येतव्यम् – अनेनाभिप्रायेण भगवता रूपाद्यायतनास्तित्वमुक्तम् न पुनः सन्त्येव तानि, यानि रूपादिविज्ञप्तीनां प्रत्येकं विषयीभवन्तीति ?

"How again one is to think that the existence of bases (of knowledge) such as colour etc., was preached by the Lord Buddha with a hidden meaning; and they are no such things which would become the subject matter of representation of consciousness of colour etc.?"

We have already explained above that the teachings of the Lord Buddha may be classified into two categories, i.e., (i) *nītārtha=pārmārthika* (direct meaning) and (ii) *neyārtha* (expedient meaning or a hidden meaning). We have also stated above that the former is meant for the higher type of disciples (*āryajana*) while the latter type of preaching is meant for the masses (*pṛthakajana*). Here what is meant is this: Lord Buddha had actually preached to the masses about the existence of the bases of knowledge (*āyatanas*) such as colour etc., but as a matter of fact, if examined from the point of consciousness, they are not mere receptacle of form and colour etc. The common man thinks that blueness is a property of an object or the object is receptacle of blueness. According to the *Vijñānavāda* in the present case the consciousness is superimposing the blueness on the object. Among the other attributes the blueness is also our mental projection on the object. This does not necessarily prove that the objects do not exist in the world. They are very much there but they really do not constitute what is colour and form. This was taught by the Lord Buddha with a hidden meaning for the masses (*pṛthakjana*).

यस्मात्

न तदेकं न चानेकं विषयः परमाणुशः

न च ते संहता यस्मात् परमाणुर्न सिध्यति ।। ११ ।।

"(The object is experienced) neither as one, nor as many atoms, nor as the atoms combined together; because the atom is not to be proved at all."

Here onwards starts Vasubandhu's criticism of realism. The criticism is based on the idea that the atomistic hypothesis is untenable as far as the perceptual experience of the various objects is concerned. The attempt on the part of Vasubandhu is mainly directed against the atomic realism of *Vaiśeṣika* system. The *Vaiśeṣika* system of philosophy had earlier accepted the objects of our experience as aggregate of atoms being the ultimate constituents. Vasubandhu is trying to hit hard the pluralism of the realists. The whole discussion is about the things in asmuch they become objects of knowledge.

The basic question is: in what mode the objects are known or experienced: as a single entity, or as many discrete atoms, or as an aggregate of atoms. Vasubandhu says that neither of the modes forms part of one's experience. Presuming an object to be white or blue, we can say that whiteness or blueness of the object is ultimately associated with the object itself. If the object (while or blue) were to consist of various atoms as the ultimate constitutents of the object, where one can locate the whiteness or blueness in the atoms when they are separated from each other. Moreover, there is a limit upto which an object can be separated from its parts and thus we see that an atom has a magnitude and yet it is composed of no further parts. The crux of the problem is the way in which the atoms get combined together.

किमुक्तं भवति ? यत् तद् रूपादिकमायतनं रूपादिविज्ञप्तीनां प्रत्येकं विषयः स्यात्, तदेकं स्यात्, यथाऽवयविरूपं कल्प्यते वैशेषिकैः अनेकं वा परमाणुशः, संहता वा त एव परमाणवः ।

"What is being said? Do the bases of knowledge (*āyatanas*) like form etc., become the object of the representation of consciousness of form etc., (as a separate entity)? Or do they become as one single entity like a (complete) whole as contemplated by the *Vaiśeṣakas*? Or do they become as many atoms? Or as aggregates of atoms?"

In the present case Vasubandhu is questioning as to what is the true mode of experience or knowing an object. Different schools of philosohy have presented different models for experience or knowing an object through the sense organ datum. Here Vasubandhu is referring to a specific model of the *Vaiśeṣikas,* who believe that the object is a conglomeration of different atoms joining together. Is an object experienced as a complete whole unit just like as the *Vaiśeṣikas* speak of an object, or is it experienced as different atoms placed apart from each other? Or an object is experienced as a conglomeration of different atoms? To say this in different words, Vasubandhu wants to know as where the form or colour is contained ? Is the form or colour contained in one atom, different atoms or in a conglomeration different atoms ?

न दावदेकं विषयो भवति । अवयवेभ्योऽन्यस्य अवयविरूपस्य क्वचिदप्यग्रहणात, नाप्यनेकम्, परमाणूनां प्रत्येकमग्रहणात्, नापि ते संहता विषयीभवन्ति, यस्मात् परमाणुरेकं द्रव्यं न सिध्यति ।

"As bases of knowledge they are not object of knowledge as a single entity because they are nowhere grasped as a complete whole different from its parts. Nor (they become object of knowledge) as many entities because no individual atom is grasped. Nor they become object of knowledge as an aggregated form; therefore, no individual atom can be proved (as a substance)."

Now onwards Vasubandhu starts a discussion concerning atoms in relation to an object. The discussion has numerous dimensions and we shall have various occasions where the different aspects concerning the atoms are gradually taken up for discussion. The basic question is: are the atoms different from the object ? Or the object is different from the atoms ? When we see an object; we see it through our eye consciousness. In the first instance the object is directly carried to our eye consciousness as a (big or small depending upon the size of the object) mass. In this mass there are various atoms constituting the object. The atoms are the parts (*avayava*) and the object is a whole (*avayavī*). At the very first sight we get the perception of the whole (*avayavī*). But in this stance the various atoms also form the part of the perception of the whole. Are all the atoms constituting this bigger whole different or separate from the whole (*avayavī*)? Such questions have been agitating the minds of different philosophers since times immemorial and each school of philosophy is trying to find out a suitable answer to this. The observations of A.K. Chatterjee are worth mentioning in this connection, "It cannot be held that what is perceived is whole, which, itself not being atomic, yet made of atoms, since no whole can be admitted over and above the atoms or the ultimate parts. So the dilemma is : the atom is not an object of perception, yet the object of perception is nothing apart from atoms."[20]

The discussion of part and whole can be illustrated by the famous example of cloth and thread. Is the cloth different from the cloth ? Are the threads different from the cloth ? Are the cloth and threads similar ? Again to quote Chatterjee, "Nor can the object be held to be a whole of parts. If there be one universal whole of which the empirical objects are parts, then it must be asked whether the latter are identical with the whole or not. If not, they cannot be created out of the latter, being different from it, if identical with it their

---

20. Chatterjee, Ashok Kumar, *The Yogācāra Idealism*, p.70.

mutual difference cannot be maintained. if the object is a whole this whole (*avayavī*) is apart from its parts (*avayavas*). Where is the cloth when the threads constituting it have been separated? How is it related to the threads ? Where does it exist ? Does it exist wholly in each of its parts or only partially so ? If the former, one part would be identical with the whole, and the rest superfluous. Then, is the whole identical with the parts or different from them ? If identical, with which part ? And moreover, if it is identical with its parts, it cannot be a separate existent apart from the. But if it is something different from the parts, it cannot be related to them, like any other set of two different. Again, some parts have some features while some have contradictory ones. A part of the cloth is in the sun and the rest in the shade. Which should be supposed to pertain to the whole ? Both cannot pertain to the same whole at the same time, for how can that be one which has oppossed characteristics?"[21]. Vasubandhu is suggesting that in any given object the hypothesis of atomistic conglomeration is highly unintelligible. In any given perceptual image the whole (*avavayī*) and the parts (*avayavas*) are taken together or rather carried to our mind through the eye consciousness. So the basic question remains: which the whole or the parts are truly the container of the object and here too its other attributes like whiteness or blueness are also to be considered simultaneously as to where these attributes of whiteness of blueness lie, whether in the whole or in parts.

कथं न सिध्यति ? यस्मात्

षट्केन युगपत्योगात् परमाणोः षडंशता ।

षड्भ्यो दिग्भ्यः षड्भि परमाणुभिर्युगपत्योगे सति परमाणोः षडंशता प्राप्नोति, एकस्य यो देश, तत्र अन्यस्यासम्भवात् ।

षण्णां समानदेशत्वात् पिण्डः स्यादणुमात्रकः ।। १२ ।।

अथ य एवैकस्य परमाणोर्देशः स एव षण्णाम्, तेन सर्वेषां समानदेशत्वात् सर्जः पिण्डः परमाणुमात्रः स्यात्, परस्पराव्यतिरेकाद इति न कश्चित् पिण्डो दृश्यः स्यात् ?

"Why (a single atom) is not proved ? Because if six atoms joining together simultaneously, an atom gets six part (ness). If there is a combination of six atoms coming from six

21. Ibid. pp.63 64.

directions; the (middle) atom gets six partness. Whatever is the place of one (atom) cannot be other's. If the six atoms belonging to the same place constitute one single mass; then that (itself) should be treated as a single atom. Whatever is the place of one atom; if the same place may belong to the sis, then on account of all (the six) atoms belonging to the same place, the whole mass would become only one atom; and on account of their being no mutual difference no such individual atom may be seen (at all)."

The believers in the existence of the reality of the objects opined that the objects consisted of various atoms joining from different directions. Vasubandhu is here examining the structure of a mass constituting different atoms. In this process there can be two possibilities. In the case of the first possibility, we have to presume that there has to be one atom in the center, (known as centroid) to which six atoms coming from six different directions would join together and thus would form a single mass. This possibility of a mass in the form of an atom being combined together with six atoms from six directions is shown below with the help of a diagram:

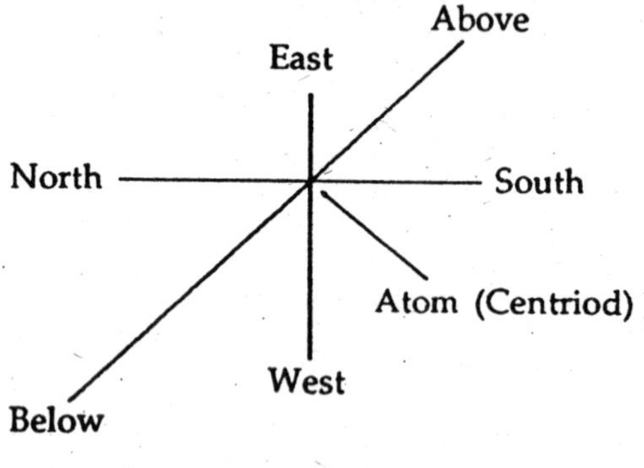

In the above diagram is shown the first possibility in which an atom (centroid shown with the mark of an arrow in the middle of the diagram) is being joined together from six directions. Now there are two positions (i) in the first position six atoms are joining the centrally placed atom from six direction; then this combination takes place from six directions, and (ii) in the second position the atoms join each other in a single direction. In the first position, when the six atoms join the centrally placed atom from six directions, then the central atom is supposed to have six parts or constituents. Thus the position of the central atom being placed in the eastern direction will not be occupied by other atoms of the rest of the directions. With the result this atom will appear to have six indivisible parts and for such an atom containing the six constituents, it would be difficult to prove it as an individual single unit in the form of a substance. In the second position when the centrally placed atom is from the eastern direction, the rest of the atoms on account of not existing in different directions, in such a position, when thousands of atoms join each other (in the same direction) even in this position there would not be any extension of this atom. With the result a mass as big as that of a mountain would also be reduced to a mere atom. So in both the positions it is very difficult to prove the existence of an atom.

The above examination of the atom from these two angles reveals that both of these positions are contradictory. In the first position there is a contradiction because it presumes that an atom has parts, whereas no atom has any parts by definition. The second one also is not tenable because that presumption fails to prove the distinction between a single atom and a collection of them.[22]

नैवं परमाणवः परस्परं संयुज्यन्ते- निरयवत्वात् मा भूद् एष दोषप्रसंगः । संहातास्तु परस्परं संयुज्यन्ते । इति काश्मीरवैभाषिकाः त इदं प्रष्टव्याः यः परमाणूनां संघातो न स तेभ्योऽर्थान्तरम् । इति,

परमाणोरसंयोगे तत्संघातेऽस्ति कस्य सः । संयोग इति वर्तते ।

"The atoms do not join each other on account of not having any parts. Let this not be (treated) as a faulty context. The *Kāśmīra* (school of) *Vaibhāṣikas* claim that the atoms join each other as aggregates. They should be asked: Whatever is

---

22. Cf.(i) संयुक्तं दूरदेशस्थं नैरन्तर्यव्यवस्थितम् ।
एकाण्वभिमुखं रूपं यदणोर्मध्यवर्त्तिनः ।।
(ii) अण्वन्तराभिमुख्येन तदेव यदि कल्प्यते ।।
प्रचयो भूधरादीनामेव सति न युज्यते ।। बहिरर्थपरीक्षा 677, 678.
(Quoted, Ram Shankar Tripathi, Vijñāptimātratāsiddhi, Varanasi, 1972, pp.49-50.

the aggregate of these atoms, this is not different from those atoms. In case of not joining these atoms; whose joining these aggregates would amount to ? The term Saṃyoga is to be understood from the context."

We have explained above that the atoms do not join each other because they do not have any parts. Further sub-division of an atom is an impossibility and this has been accepted as a norm in philosophy. We are not talking here of physical sciences where there is every possibility of further dividing an atom into hundreds of them. This division of an atom may produce a lot of energy in science but not in philosophy. Vasubandhu is referring to a sub-sect of the *Vaibhāṣikas* known as *Kāśmīra Vaibhāṣikas*. According to them the atoms join each other as aggregates. Vasubandhu questions them as far as this viability is concerned. He asks: is this joining of the atoms as aggregates different from the atoms themselves ? Here also the basic question remains the same: whether the mass of atoms is different from the atoms or is the same ? In case you do not subscribe to the view that the atoms join each other; then whose joining can be attributed to their aggregates.

न चानवयवत्वेन तत्संयोगे न सिध्यति ।। १३ ।।

अथ संघाता अप्यन्योऽन्यं संयुज्यन्ते, न तर्हि परमाणूनां निरव्यवत्वात् संयोगो न सिध्यतीति वक्तव्यम्,

सावयवस्यापि हि संघातस्य संयोगानभ्युगमनात् ।

तस्मात् परमाणुरेकं द्रव्यं न सिध्यति ।

"The joining of atoms cannot be proved on account of their not having parts. (If you say that) the aggregates of atoms do not join each other; then it must be said that the joining of the atoms is not be proved on account of their not having any parts. There is no joining of aggregates of atoms even if they have parts. Therefore, the atoms cannot be proved as a single substance."

Vasubandhu has made it clear uptil now that the atomic conceptual image of an object does not make any sense. It is rather endowed with numerous apparent contradictions which are very difficult to solve. As already explained, combination of atoms is possible only in two ways. Atoms join each other from six directions and secondly atoms join each other from one single direction. In the first instance, if the atoms join each other from different directions, then the atom itself in subject to the condition of having the six parts, which is an absurdity. In the second instance, when the atoms join each other is a single direction, then the whole mass or the object is reduced to a single atom. Thus both these cases are basically untenable because in both the cases it is very difficult to prove the very existence of the atom.

यदि च परमाणोः संयोग इष्यते, यदि वा नेष्यते, दिग्भागभेदो यस्यास्ति तस्यैकत्वं न युज्यते ।

अन्यो हि परमाणोः पूर्वदिग्भागो यावदधोदिग्भाग सति दिग्भागभेदे कथं तदात्मकस्य परमाणोरेकत्वं योक्ष्यते ।

"If the joining of the atoms is desired or is not desired; (then) an atom having a differentiation of directions, the joining of such an atom is not appropriate. The atom (coming) from the eastern direction is different and (from here onwards) that part of the atom (coming from western direction or the lower part) is different. When such varieties in relations to different directions exist; how there can be the appropriateness of unity of such an atom ?"

Vasubandhu examines atomic conceptual image of a mass from the directional point of view. Here the basic issue is: when one atom is supposed to come from the upper or the eastern direction, another atom is supposed to come from the lower part. In such a situation how can you talk of the appropriateness of the unity of the atoms. To Vasubandhu it is either a case of extension or a single mass in the form of an object. In both the cases there are practical difficulties.

छायावृती कथं वा

यद्येकैकस्य परमाणोर्दिग्भागभेदो न स्यात्, आदित्योदये कथमन्यत्र छाया भवति, अन्यत्र आतपः । न हि तस्यान्यः प्रदशोऽस्ति यत्रातपो न स्यात् ।

आवरणं च कथं भवति, परमाणोः परमाण्वन्तरेण यदि दिग्भागभेदो नेष्यते । न हि कश्चिदपि हि परमाणोः परभागोऽस्ति, यत्रागमनादन्येनान्यस्य प्रतिघातः स्यात् । असति च प्रतिघाते सर्वेषां समानदेशत्वात् सर्वः संघातः परमाणुमात्रः स्यादित्युक्तम् ।

"How can there be shadow and cover ? If the each atom did not have directional differentiation, how could there be at one place shadow at sunrise, and sunshine at another place (at the sunrise). Because an atom does not have other side where there would be no sunshine. If there is directional differentiation in relation to with the other; how there can be any cover ? No atom has any other directional side, where the arrival of one atom would be obstructed by another. In the absence of any obstruction and all the atoms belonging to the same place, an aggregate of atoms would be reduced to a mere atom, this has already been said."

Vasubandhu is trying to base his arguments on one important factor i.e., that an atom is an indivisible unit by its very nature. In this connection any extension or extensionlessness of this atom has no significant consideration for our purpose. If such a situation is accepted in relation to an atom; then one part of it would be exposed in shadow and another part out of shadow. You cannot visualise any object or a mass of which one side would be exposed to light and another to shadow. If the directional differentiation is not accepted, then how could one atom be covered by the other ? Similarly an atom does not have any other part or side where one atom becomes obstructed by the arrival of another. This position leads us to a point where there is no obstruction of one atom by another. All the atoms are supposed to belong to a similar place; the whole aggregate of atom by itself. This is a very moot point which has been discussed earlier also. Such a position of an atom only shows that the atom remains a single indivisible unit of which no further dissection is possible. Vasubandhu argues that those who believe in the reality of the objects of the world are only suggesting an impossibility. Even earlier also some of the philosophical schools had shown that what appears in the form of an atom is a conglomeration of atoms. This is an atomic conceptualisation of the universe as suggested by Vasubandhu's opponents.

किमेवं नेष्यते पिण्डस्य ते छायावृती न परमाणोरिति ? किं खलु परमाणुभ्योऽन्यः पिण्ड इष्यते, यस्य ते स्याताम् । न इत्याह ।

अन्यो न पिण्डश्चेन्न तस्य ते ।। १४ ।।

यदि नान्यः परमाणुभ्यः पिण्ड इष्यते, न ते तस्येति सिद्धं भवति॰।

"Why do you not accept the shadow and the cover to belong to the mass and not to the atom ? Do you accept the mass as different from the atoms, whose shadow and cover they are ? It is said that it is not so. If the mass is not different from the atom, then they (shadow and cover) cannot belong to it (mass). If you think that the mass is not different from the atom; then these the shadow and the cover do not belong to the mass this has been proved."

The realists are trying to prove that the atomic conceptualisation of the universe or an object is a reality and it should be accepted. The *Vijñānavādins* are objecting to it in order to demolish the edifice built by the realists in the form of atoms constituting a mass. The realists say that how does it matter whether the mass is an aggregate of atoms or not. They simply say that this is an induced imagination. What they wish to suggest is this: a mass constituting of numerous atoms is a peculiar situation (*sanniveṣa parikalpa eṣah*).

सन्निवेषपरिकल्प एषः । परमाणुसंघात इति वा, किमनया चिन्तया, लक्षणं तु रूपादि यदि न प्रतिषिध्यते । किं पुनस्तेषां लक्षणम् ? चक्षुरादिविषयं नीलादित्वं च । तदेवैदं सम्प्रधार्यते यत्तच्चक्षुरादीनां विषयो नीलपीतादिकमिष्यते, कि तदेकं द्रव्यमथवा तदनेकमिति ?

"This is a peculiar situation. Whether it is an aggregate or an atom, how does it matter if the characteristics of the atom etc., is not to be obstructed. What again is their definition ? Whether it is their being the object of eye etc., there being blue. That verily is to be determined. That is, blue, yellow etc., are supposed to be (or desired) as objects of eye etc., Whether that object is (to be treated) as a single substance or to be treated as manifold substances."

The *Sautrāntikas,* who believe in the reality of the object say that in every case of a mass, there is a peculiar situation of the atoms. Normally an example is given of a circle where atoms are placed discretely, where every atom is not a circle but the whole mass is definitely constituted of numerous atoms. It must be remembered that all the numerous atoms constituting the circle do not possess the causal efficiency (*arthakriyākāritva*). Thus while sub-dividing this mass one reaches a stage, which may be designated as atom. When all these atoms are placed in a peculiar position, they assume the shape of a particular object. But the point raised by the *Sautrāntikas* is that while discussing the positions of different atoms either in the form of aggregate or otherwise, the basic form or the characteristics of an object is not denied at all. The opponents maintain a view: how does it matter whether a single atom forms the object of consciousness or the aggregate forms the object of consciousness. With the result the colour etc., of different objects remains there very much as entities and thus the position of those who maintain the reality of the objects remains unchanged. Then question is brought into the discussion: what is the object of eye etc., whether it is the object or the colours like blue yellow etc. A further extension of this is whether : (whatever) forms the object of consciousness, (atoms or aggregate) the object of the eye etc., is one or many.

किं चातः ?

अनेकत्वे दोष उक्तः ।

एकत्वे न क्रमेणेतिर्युगपन्न ग्रहाग्रहौ ।

विछिन्नानेकवृत्तिश्च सूक्ष्मानीक्षा च नो भवेत् ।। १५ ।।

यदि यावदविच्छिन्नं नानेकं चक्षुषो विषयस्तदेकं द्रव्यं कल्प्यते, पृथिव्यां क्रमेणेतिर्न गमनमित्यर्थः । सकृत्पादक्षेपेण सर्वस्य गतत्वात् ।

अर्वाग्भागस्य च ग्रहणं परभागस्य चाग्रहणं युगपन्न स्यात्, न हि तस्यैव तदानीं ग्रहणं चाग्रणं च युक्तम् ।

विच्छिन्नस्य चानेकस्य हस्त्यश्वादिकस्यैकत्र वृत्तिर्न स्याद् यत्रैव ह्येकं तत्रैवापरमिति कथं तयोर्विच्छेद इष्यते । कथं वा तदेकं यत् प्राप्तं च, ताभ्यां न च प्राप्तम्, अन्तराले तच्छून्यग्रहणात् ।

सूक्ष्माणां चौदकजन्तूनां स्थूलैः समानरूपाणामनीक्षणं न स्यात् ।

यदि लक्षणभेदादेव द्रव्यान्तरत्वं कल्प्यते, नान्यथा । तस्मादवश्यं परमाणुशो भेदः कल्पयितव्यः स चैको न सिध्यति । तस्यासिद्धौ रूपादीनां चक्षुरादिविषयत्व-मसिद्धमिति सिद्धं विज्ञप्तिमात्रं भवतीति ।

"What is the purpose of this question ? The fault as has already been shown in case of many substances (or entities) (being the objects of eye consciousness). (In case whole of the earth being treated as a) single substance or unit, there would be neither progressive movement nor simultaneous grasping and non-grasping. Nor there would be differentiation (or different states) nor there should be different states, and there would be not any minute observation (of the subtle beings). If the earth were to be imagined as one single entity or object of the eye, and not many, there would not be any progressive movement, the word *'iti'* means walking or movement; because one would be able to traverse the whole world just by one step. (Moreover), the simultaneous grasping of the front side (of a thing) and the non-grasping of the back side (of a thing) would not be there; because the grasping of a thing at a particular moment and non-grasping of the same thing is not possible (or appropriate). Different and many elephants, horse etc., cannot occupy the same place, because wherever there is one (elephant), how there can be another (horse); (in such a position) how can one talk of their separation ? How can it be that one which is accessible there and that very one is not accessible by two others because in between the empty space is also to be obtained then if substances are to be imagined (or distinguished) only on the basis of definition, and not otherwise, the tiny aquatic bacteria being equal in form (or size) would not be invisible. Therefore, you must accept the difference between the atoms, and that atom (as a single) unit is not be proved (at all). In such a case if it not being proved, it is proved that form etc., are not the objects of eye etc., and thus the mere representation of consciousness becomes proved."

We have observed until now that Vasubandhu's criticism is against the realism of the *Sautrāntikas* and also the *Vaiśeṣikas*, who believe in the atomic realism. During the course of this criticism, we have seen that Vasubandhu has proved that if this universe were to consist of many discrete atoms then, such an atomic conceptualised image of the world is an impossibility. This was one aspect of the problem. He takes up the second aspect of the problem i.e., if the entire universe were to be treated as a single unit (basically thereby meaning that the entire universe were to be treated like a single atom); then there are numerous difficulties in this proposition. Our experience shows that such a situation in which the entire earth were to be treated like a single unit, is basically unintelligible because there cannot be simultaneous grasping and non-grasping of the entire earth. From here onwards starts the minute criticism of realism by Vasubandhu from various point of views. As already said above, (i) let us imagine that this entire universe is a flat one; can there be any progressive movement possible in such a position because one step would not be able to traverse the entire earth, (ii) moreover, if this universe is to be treated as a single unit like a wall etc. It is impossible to grasp it from one side and it cannot be grasped from another side simultaneously. There cannot be a simultaneous grasping and non-grasping (iii) if the entire earth were to be treated like a single unit or a whole: there would be no discrete states of many beings; because all of them would be occupying the only single space available. In such a situation, on the earth an elephant is standing, a horse should also occupy the same earth or should stand there itself. Vasubandhu makes a further extension of this argument. How can this entire earth were to be a single (partless) whole, whose one part is occupied by the elephant and the same part is unoccupied by the horse likewise the part occupied by the horse is unoccupied by the elephant. With the result an earth occupied by the elephant and unoccupied by the horse simultaneously such as earth can never be a single substance or a single whole. Moreover, the elephant occupies a specific portion of the earth and the horse occupies another specific portion of the earth and in between some empty space also is left out. (iv) Vasubandhu gives the fourth argument in order to disprove the 'atomic realism'. He says that if blue, yellow etc., were to be the objects of the eye consciousness as a single whole unit then the tiny aquatic bacteria (which is visible only through the scientific instrument like microscope) will be visible as any other major thing like mountain etc., because all beings of the some size, then there would not be any distinguishing feature between gross and subtle beings and between visible and invisible things. He ends his criticism of atomic realism by saying that the atoms are to be distinguished as discrete atom. It is very difficult to prove the identity or existence of a single atom. It must be noted that Vasubandhu has thrice repeated the statement, i.e., an atom is not to be proved (i) *Viṃśatikā, Kārikā*,11, (ii) *Viṃśatikā Vṛtti* 11, and (iii) *Viṃśatikā, Kārikā*, 13). Kochumuttom translates the term '*sidhyati*' as is obtained' and he says, "To be sure, the term does not mean 'to exist (*asti*). Therefore, to translate the above sentence as an atom does not exist would be a gross mistake. The usual meanings of the term '*sidhyati*' are to be obtained (in experience) to be given, (in experience) or 'to be proved to be true etc."[23] Vasubandhu's main charge against atomic realism is that they are neither given in experience to be proved to be as such. It must also be observed that the whole discussion is carried out in the context of knowledge and existence only. Our mode of experience of the objects of the world is only their perceptual image. If this perceptual image of the objects is to consist of the atomic realism; then it stands nowhere when subjected to the experiential knowledge relating to the objects in our day-to-day life. Vasubandhu objects to this mode of experience where the atomic realism is taken into consideration whereas no single atom, nor many discrete atoms and nor the aggregates of them are experienced at all in our life. What we perceive is the direct object with our eye consciousness; the object is always endowed with the other attributes but the eye consciousness sees the object as a single whole. It is really very difficult to separate the object from the other properties or attributes, i.e., white, blue etc. Our experience shows that our mode of perceiving the object is a direct one. There is nothing in between the eye and the object. The object is carried to the eye consciousness alongwith its other properties or attributes. This whole discussion reveals that in the composition of an object the atoms definitely play a very important role but this is only a conglomeration of the atoms. Vasubandhu is to prove that the existence of an atom, whether singularly or collectively in the form of the aggregates is basically untenable and no mode of experience can prove the existence of an atom. Kochumuttom observes, "Vasubandhu's thesis that objects insofar as they are experienced, are subjective forms of consciousness, and therefore comparable to objects experienced in dreams, stands. It would mean that an ordinary man's experience of extension, movement, partial knowledge, shadow and concealment, quantity, difference, relation etc., etc., have all to be real, and corresponding to the extra mental world. But, as Vasubandhu has shown, atomic realism cannot in any way explain, or account for, such experience".[24]

---

23. Kochumuttom Thomas A, A. Buddhist Doctrine of Experience, op.cit., p.180. (Here he quotes. C.H. Homilton, who translates this term *'sidhyati'* as "is proved".
24. Ibid., pp.100-101.

परमाणुवशादस्तित्वं नास्तित्वं वा निर्धार्यते, सर्वेषां च प्रत्यक्षं प्रमाणं गरिष्ठमित्यसत्यर्थे कथमियं बुद्धिर्भवति प्रत्यक्षम् इति ।

"Existence and non-existence are to be determined on the basis of (valid) means of knowledge. Of all the means of knowledge (direct) perception is the best. Then in the absence of an object, how does one acquire the knowledge 'a thing is being perceived by me.'".

Now Vasubandhu's criticism of realism comes to an end. It is quite clear from the arguments given in this regard that the *Sautrāntikas* have so far failed in their arguments in support of the theory of reality of external objects, whereas on the other hand Vasubandhu has very successfully met their arguments. It must be admitted to the credit of Vasubandhu that he has almost brought his opponents to a virtual collapse. Thus realising the *Sautrāntikas* that they can no longer argue further in the debate, i.e., they now try to bring in the case of the perception of the object. Having virtually failed in all other modes of arguments, his opponents come to the mundane level of argument. According to them, it is the sense perception (of an eye) of the object, which is recognised as a best means of knowledge among all other means of knowledge. When one directly sees an object, one gets the awareness that, 'I have seen the objects'. This process rather confirms that the eye has a direct perception of the object alongwith all the other properties or attributes. The *Sautrāntikas* mean that the eye (consciousness) directly sees the form colour etc., of the object in the form of external reality. They suggest that this leaves no doubt about the validity of the external object because such an awareness is created by the best possible means of a valid knowledge. This is what is indirectly known as subject-object relationship of knowledge, i.e., a subject having a corresponding unit in the form of an object in the world. The following passage shows that Vasubandhu is interested in refuting the correspondence theory of knowledge. His argument against the theory of knowledge is drawn again from the illusory dream experiences.

प्रत्यक्षबुद्धिः स्वप्नादौ यथा
विनाप्यर्थेनेति पूर्वमेव ज्ञापितम् ।
सा च यदा तदा ।

न सोऽर्थो दृश्यते तस्य प्रत्यक्षत्वं कथं मतम् ।। १६ ।।

यदा च सा प्रत्यक्षबुद्धिर्भवति- 'इदं मे प्रत्यक्षम्' इति तदा न सोऽर्थो दृश्यते मनोविज्ञानेनैव परिच्छेदात्, चक्षुर्विज्ञानस्य च तदा निरुद्धत्वादिति कथं प्रत्यक्षत्वमिष्टम्, विशेषेण तु क्षणिकस्य विषयस्य तदानीं निरुद्धमेव ततद् रुपं रसादिकं वा ।

"Perception occurs in dream etc., - even without the object (being there) has already been discussed. When that perception takes place, that object is not visible, how one can talk of its perception ? When this direct perception takes place 'This is being (directly) perceived by me' - then that object is not visible because the mind-consciousness is obstructed and the eye-consciousness is also obstructed, how that direct perception is desired specially when the object is momentary and at that time form and colour etc., (of the object) are also obstructed."

When the *Sautrāntikas* have almost exhausted all the arguments against the *Vijñānavādins* in order to prove the reality of the external objects, they try to bring in the mode of direct perception as a valid means of knowledge to prove the existence of object. Vasubandhu maintains that the question of direct perception has already been discussed previously and that too without the object being present over there. But his opponents are not satisfied with this. Vasubandhu asks: when the object is not seen at all, how can you talk of its perception ? What is really a perception ? Perception is the reflective awareness of the object that I have seen the object. Here Vasubandhu realises various stages of perception in which it takes place. He suggests that when the perception occurs our perceptive faculty or the reflective faculty comes into contact with the object. The whole process works like this. First, the eye consciousness (which is the objective basis, i.e., *ālambanapratyaya*) comes into contact with the object in the first moment. In the second place, one knows through the reflective process that he has had the perception of the object. This happens in the second moment. Herein Vasubandhu brings in certain difficulties in the process of perception. When the eye consciousness comes into contact with the object, this is the first moment and there is no reflective process. When the perceptive faculty or the reflective process takes place in the second moment, there is no contact with the object because this happens in the second instance. It is quite evident that when this second moment comes in, the first one has already disappeared. According to Vasubandhu the perception takes place in the second moment when the eye is no longer in contact with the object. He gives two reasons for this defective process of perception i.e., (i) in the first place the (stream) of mind consciousness is broken (*mano-vijñānena eva paricchedāt*), (ii) secondly at this stage the eye consciousness is also obstructed (*cakṣur vijñānasya ca tadā nirudhatvāt iti*). According to him the perception takes place only by the thought consciousness. Moreover, in the second moment when the eye consciousness is virtually contemplating the object, this object is really *nirvikalpa* (without any form). At that time, it has no power to determine as to that this is the external object.[25] In addition to the two above mentioned objections against the perception, Vasubandhu raises another objection i.e., that of the momentariness. If the form and colour etc., of the object are capable of being present in the second moment; they can be grasped but because of being momentary they cannot remain in the second moment. Since they are not in a position to stay until the second moment, they cannot become the object of the eye consciousness. Here Vasubandhu observes that when it is impossible for the perception to grasp the object, then the mind projects or rather creates the object through its mental faculty known as consciousness. It is this mental thought consciousness which is superimposed on the object. Thus according to Vasubandhu only the consciousness is real and the external objects are unreal. In this way Vasubandhu has replied to all the objections of the defenders of the correspondence theory of knowledge.

नाननुभूतं मनोविज्ञानेन स्मर्यत इत्यवश्यमर्थानुभवेन भवितव्यम्, तच्च दर्शनमित्येवं तद् विषयस्य रूपादेः प्रत्यक्षत्वं मतम् ।

असिद्धमिदमनुभूतस्यार्थस्य स्मरणं भवतीति, यस्मात् उक्तं यथा तदाभासा विज्ञप्तिः विनाप्यर्थेन यथार्थभासा

25. Cf. *Pramāṇavārtikam*, 239-240, ed. Dwarkadass Shastri, Varanasi, 1984, pp.172-173; पूर्वानुभूत ग्रहणे मानस्याप्रमाणता ।
अदृष्टग्रहणेऽन्धादेरपि स्यादर्थदर्शनम् ।।
क्षणिकत्वादतीतस्य दर्शनस्व न सम्भवः ।।
वाच्यमक्षणिकत्वे स्याल्लक्षणं सविशेषणम् ।।

चक्षुर्विज्ञानादिका विज्ञप्तिरुत्पद्यते तथोक्तम् ।

(स्मरणं ततः) ।

ततो हि विज्ञप्तेः स्मृतिसम्प्रयुक्ता तत्प्रतिभासैव रूपादिविकल्पिका मनोविज्ञप्तिरूत्पद्यत इति न स्मृत्युत्पाददर्थानुभवः सिध्यति ।

"(Something) inexperienced is not remembered by the thought consciousness. Therefore, the object must be necessarily experienced and that (direct) vision should make the colour etc., (as its) objects (of the memory). It is not proved that experienced object becomes remembered because it has been said (already) that there is a representation of consciousness appearing (as if accompanying) the objects. So it has been said that even without the objects being there arises a representation of consciousness i.e., eye consciousness appearing (as if accompanying) the object. From it does follow the memory. From that representation of consciousness arises a mind consciousness associating memory with it appearing as if accompanying the object discriminating the colour, object etc. (So) the production of the memory does not prove the experience of an object."

The *Sautrāntikas*, having almost failed in their endeavour to defend the reality of the external object bring in the concept of memory which is also associated with the experience of the object. They say that things inexperienced cannot be remembered by the mind consciousness. This leads to a position in which the object is directly perceived as colour, form etc. They explain the whole process like this. At the time, when memory takes place, our mind is not at all in direct touch with the external object. But it must be noted that at one stage the mind was definitely in touch with the object thus giving rise to an experience which in its own way makes the memory possible. The *Vijñānavādins* do not accept this position. According to them the objects are not remembered by memory because it has already been discussed previously that there is a representation of consciousness appearing (as if accompanying) the object. The *Vijñānavādins* maintain that the representation of consciousness arises even without the object being present. In such a situation a special type of consciousness associated with the sense organ of the eye arises giving the impression of an object. It is exactly here from where the memory follows. So it is proved that mere memory does not necessiate the presence of the external objects. Then a mind consciousness is also produced discriminating the colour and form etc. The memory is not in any way associated with the experience and the uprising of the memory does not necessarily prove the experience of the object.

यदि यथा स्वप्ने विज्ञप्तिरभूतार्थाविषया तथा जाग्रतोऽपि स्यात् तथैव तदभावं लोकः स्वयमवगच्छेत् न चैवं भवति, तस्मान्न स्वप्न इवार्थोपलब्धिः सर्वाः निरर्थका ।

इदमज्ञापकम्, यस्मात्

स्वप्ने दृग्विषयाभावं नाप्रतिबुद्धोऽवगच्छति ।। १७ ।।

एवं वितथविकल्पाभ्यासवासनानिद्रया प्रसुप्तो लोकः स्वप्न इवाभूतमर्थं पश्यन्नप्रबुद्धस्तदभावं यथावन्नावगच्छति । यदा तु तत्प्रतिपक्षलोकोत्तरनिर्विकल्पज्ञानलाभात् प्रबुद्धो भवति तदा तत्पृष्ठलब्धशुद्धलौकिकज्ञानसम्मुखीभावाद् विषयाभावं यथावदवगच्छतीति समानमेतत् ।

"If in a dream the representation of consciousness is unrealistic, then if the same be true in a waking state, the world may understand the absence of the objects in a similar manner; but this really does not happen. Therefore, not all perceptions are objectless just like a dream. This does not make any sense; because in a dream one does not feel the absence of the objects unless one is awake. Similarly the world (thereby meaning a common man) asleep by the habit of conceptual construction in the form of different impressions just like a dream seeing the unrealistic objects does not really know their absence unless he is awake. When, however, he is awake by acquiring the supra-mundane and non-discrimination knowledge; he really gains the absence of the objects by putting down (or giving up) the previously acquired, impure mundane knowledge. Thus the dream knowledge and the waking knowledge are similar."

The *Sautrāntikas,* taking the clue from the dream experience intend to prove that because there are no objects in the dreams, similarly in the walking states also there are no objects corresponding to different concepts. But as far as the mundane experience is concerned, this is not really so. It must be pointed out that Vasubandhu is suggesting here two different models with regard to the theory of knowledge. The present context is very much important because it tries to explain as to how we get the two different types of knowledge of different objects of the world. Vasubandhu, it appears, is talking of a two-way reflex action process of knowledge.[26]

In the first place the nomeclature of the external object is carried to the mind. When this happens, at this point of time, this is pure and the mundane type of knowledge (*śuddha laukika jñāna*). To this Vasubandhu adds that another adjective i.e., *pṛṣṭhalabdha* (previously acquired knowledge). This is the previous stage of knowing the object in which we are confronted with the object. This is the mundane knowledge and this is also in its purest form. This is a situation in which most of the ordinary masses are normally placed in and they do not have the capacity to transcend this position. Vasubandhu very tacitly compares this position with deep sleep of the masses (*nidrayā prasupta lokaḥ*). Moreover, Vasubandhu points out the usual habit of the masses of creating the conceptual construction or the subjective activity of thought interpreting the object (*vikalpa abhyāsavāsanā*). To put it differently, we say that in our day-to-day routine life, we try to put different lables or names on different objects of the world without knowing their reality. As a matter of fact, we have no means of knowledge available to us to ascertain the real nature of things. Vasubandhu is comparying this situation with a dream (experience), Kochumuttom remarks, "What Vasubandhu suggests here is that the dream experience is to be taken only as model towards understanding the entire Saṃsāric experience".[27] This is a situation in which we are unable to realise that these objects are only created by our mental images. This is a situation comparable with deep sleep. Vasubandhu suggests a higher stage of enlightenment in which one is able to transcend the sleep and realise that what he has taken for realities, were only imaginary dream objects.

---

26. (i) Sharma, T.R. 'Śantideva's' Criticism of Vijñānavāda and Bodhicatta", *Glory of Knowledge*, Prof. Ram Murti Sharma Felicitation Vol., Delhi, 1990, p.202. (ii) Uttartantra of Maitreyā 2.7, ed. Prashad, H.S. Delhi, 1991, p.148: द्वयावरणविश्लेषहेतुर्ज्ञान द्वयं पुनः ।
निर्विकल्पं च तत्पृष्ठलब्धं तन्ज्ञानमिष्यते ।।
(iii) Āsyāsaṅga commentory on Ibid, p.147:
द्विविधं ज्ञानं लोंकोत्तरमविकल्पं तत्पृष्ठलब्धं च ।
(iv) Ibid. p.150:
यत्तु द्विविधं लोकोत्तरमविकल्पं तत्पृष्ठलब्धं च ज्ञानमाश्रयपरिविवृत्तेर्हेतुसंयोगफलसंशितायाः।।
27. Kochumuttom, op.cit., p.186.

This is a higher type of supra mundane non-discriminating knowledge. When one gains this type of special knowledge, one immediately realises that until now he was sleepy in the world and all the objects which he was taking as real, were only his mental creations or imaginary objects. To rise above to this stage is really to become awake in the world. A.K. Chatterjee says, "Idealism holds that all, over empirical experience is of the nature of a dream. Just as in the latter experience of things appear as existing in space and time and yet have no existence apart from their being experienced, so in the case of our waking experience as well."[28] When one realises that all the mundane objects are only unreal objects in reality, he realises this in a similar manner of dream experience also. Vasubandhu maintains that this is similar in both cases, viz., dreaming and the waking stage. According to him when one is awakened through the acquisition of such a supra mundane and non-discriminating knowledge, the previously acquired impure mundane knowledge vanishes immediately. To quote Kochumuttom, "Thus, what he (Vasubandhu) says is that the individuals in that state of Saṃsāra are in a cosmic slumber, which makes them dream so many objects. Mental images as they are, those dream-objects are mistaken for things-in-themselves by the unenlightened".[29] From this it may be concluded that the dreaming and waking experience are the same.

यदि स्वसन्तानपरिणामविशेषादेव सत्वानामर्थप्रतिभासा विज्ञप्तयः उत्पद्यन्ते, नार्थविशेषात्, तदा य एष कल्याणमित्रसम्पर्कात् सदसद्धर्मश्रवणाच्च विज्ञप्तिनियमः सत्वानां स कथं सिद्धयति, असति सदसत्सम्पर्के तद्देशनायां च ?

अन्योऽन्याधिपतित्वेन विज्ञप्तिनियमो मिथः ।

सर्वेषां हि सत्वानामन्योऽन्यविज्ञप्त्याधिपत्येन मिथो निज्ञप्तेर्नियिमो भवति यथायोगम् । मिथ इति परस्परतः । अतः सन्तानान्तरविज्ञप्तिविशेषात् सन्तानान्तरे विज्ञप्तिर्विशेष उत्पद्यते, नार्थविशेषात् ।

"If the representations of consciousness appearing (in

28. Chatterjee, A.K., op.cit. p.78.
29. Kochumuttom, op.cit., p.187.

the form of) objects are produced due to particular transformation of streams of the respective beings, and not due to particular (external) object; then how it is proved that a representation of consciousness is determined by contacts with bad or good friends and by listening to right or wrong teachings, even though there would be no contacts with good or bad friends and their teachings ?

The law of representation of consciousness is proved by mutual influence of one individual over the other. The law of representation of consciousness of all (being) is proved due to the mutual influence of the representation of consciousness of one individual over the other repectively. The term *'mithaḥ;* means mutual. Therefore, on account of a particular representation of consciousness of one stream is produced a particular representation of consciousness in another stream and not due to (any) particular object."

A study of this concluding part of the text i.e., *Viṃśatikā* shows that Vasubandhu here talks of inter-actions and inter-relations between individuals influencing consciousness. While doing so, he admits plurality of beings at the phenomenal level. From the context it is also clear that Vasubandhu talks of social relations of the individuals. When we study the present portion of the text, we find that discussion is about as to how far the consciousness of the different individuals affect each other. At the phenemenal level, according to Vasubandhu the consciousness of one individual is able to influence the consciousness of another individual. In order to prove this he uses a word, i.e., *anyo 'nyādhipati.'* Candrakīrti says in *Prasannapadā* says that the term *'adhipati'* means by presence of something, something else happens.[30] This shows that the consciousness of one individual is associated with another and they are able to influence each other. The stream of consciousness of one individual is also able to influence the stream of another. Thus the inter-relation of the stream of individuals causes the particular consciousness to be produced. In this connection the remarks of Kochumuttom are worth mentioning, "Here, on the one hand, the question is about how people influence each other, and now their character is affected by mutual friendship, conversation etc. This question invariably

30. Cf. Candrakīrti's *Prasannapadā* on Madhyamakaśāstra 1.4. ed. Dwarkadass Shastri, Varanasi, 1983, p 29: यस्मिन् सति यद्भवति तत्तस्याधिपतेयमिति ।

presumes a multiplexity of really existing individuals. The only genuine problem in this regard is how these individuals, whose ultimate natures are ineffable and is incommunicable, can reach each other in order to influence each other. About objects of knowledge Vasubandhu said that they are nothing extra-mental, but only mental images. But when he says that two individuals influence each other in one way or the other, he must mean that they are really existing beings. Thus Vasubandhu clearly admits that there are different individuals inter-acting and influencing each other. But since he believes that the real nature of each individual is inaccessible and incommunicable, he must explain how the inter-relation and mutual influencing of individuals is possible. This is what he does in the stanzas under discussion. His explanation may be put as follows. The real nature of individuals is ineffable, inaccessible and uncommunicable. But in their phenomenal nature they are, and act like individual streams of mental energy, which can influence and affect each other. In other words, each individual is somewhat determined by other individual streams of mental energy, although the ultimate nature of all of them would always remain untouched."[31] From this it follows that the stream of consciousness of different individuals mutually influence each other and they are also inter connected. It must be noted that the particular objects do not play any role as far as the consciousness of the various individuals is concerned.

यदि यथा स्वप्ने निरर्थका विज्ञप्तिरेवं जाग्रतोऽपि स्यात्, कस्मात् कुशलाकुशलसमुदाचारे सुप्तासुप्तयोस्तुल्यं फलमिष्टामिष्टमायत्यां न भवति ?

यस्मात्

मिद्धेनोपहतं चित्तं स्वप्ने तेनासमं फलम् ।। १८ ।।

इदमत्र कारणम्, न त्वर्थसद्भावः ।

यदि विज्ञप्तिमात्रमेवेदम्, न कस्यचित् कायोऽस्ति, न वाक्, कथमुपक्रम्यमाणानामौरभ्रिकादिभिरूरभ्रादीनां मरणं भवति । अतत्कृते वा मरणे कथमौरभ्रिकादीनां प्राणातिपातावद्येन योगो भवति ?

"If the representation of consciousness in a waking stage

---

31. Kochumutton, op.cit., p.190.

were to be without the object like a dream, then how is it that the good and bad actions of a dreamer and a waking man, do not have the desired and undersired fruits in future ? Because; in a dream the mind is overpowered by sleepiness, therefore, there are unequal results. This is the reason, and not the existence of the (external) objects. If this were to be mere representation of consciousness, there is no one's body and no body's word. Then how the death could happen to the goat by the butcher ? Even when that might not be done by (the butcher) or (the goat) might not be killed by (the butcher), how is it that the butcher is blamed with the sin of killing the goat ?"

In our study earlier we have seen that the dreams play an important role in our life. It was also shown earlier that the whole of our life is just a dream. According to Vasubandhu this is characterised by sleepiness or ignorance (*middha*). Apart from this there is no difference between the waking and the dreaming stage. The *Sautrāntikas,* who believe in the reality of the external objects, are not satisfied with a situation in which the waking and the dreaming stage is the same. They are raising an important point with regard to the actions done in the waking stage and dreaming stage. They say that one's experience in waking and dreaming stages are the same. According to their view point, it may be argued that as far as the dreaming stage is concerned, no body is held responsible for what he does in dream. But when it comes to the waking stage, everybody has to accept the responsibility of whatever he does when he is awake. To this Vasubandhu replies that during the dream the mind is always overpowered with sleepiness and on account of this sleepiness there are unequal results in the world. Not satisfied with this *Sautrāntikas* raise the phenomenal question of death. In case of death caused by the butcher, one hand is raised and he is asked to kill the goat by somebody else. If, as accepted by the *Vijñānavādins,* the whole process of death is only a mental representation, how is it that the butcher is accused of killing the animal. It must be noted that the debate between the *Sautrāntikas* and the *Vijñānavādins* is concerned with the down-to-earth question of death. One may accept for the time being that real existing objects are mental images of one's own consciousness but one cannot easily set aside the brutal question of goat's death being caused by a butcher. This was really a challenge posed by Vasubandhu's opponents, i.e., the

Sautrāntikas, who all along have been fighting tooth and nail in order to prove the reality of the external objects. Kochumuttom says in this connection, "If Vasubandhu were an idealist or a monist or both, he should not have taken this objection seriously. Instead he could very easily dismiss it saying that nobody kills anybody in the real sense of the term. But this is not the way Vasubandhu faces this question. On the contrary, tacitly admitting that there are real beings who can kill each other, he is trying to give a new explanation to the phenomena of death an explanation that will fit in well with his philosophical system."[32]

मरणं परविज्ञप्तिविशेषाद् विक्रिया यथा ।
स्मृतिलोपादिकान्येषां पिशाचादिमनोवशात् ।। १९ ।।

यथा हि पिशाचादिमनोवशादन्येषां स्मृतिलोप-स्वप्रदर्शन- भूतग्रहावेशविकारा भवन्ति, ऋद्धिवन्मनोवशाच्च, यथा सारणस्यार्यमहकात्यानाधिष्ठानात् स्वप्रदर्शनम् आरण्यकर्षिमनःप्रदोषाञ्च वेमचित्रपराजयः तथा परविज्ञप्ति-विशेषाधिपत्यात् परेषां जीवितेन्द्रियविरोधिनी काचिद् विक्रियोत्पद्यते, यया सभागसन्ततिविच्छेदाख्यं मरणं भवतीति वेदितव्यम् ।

"Death is transformation caused by a particular consciousness of another being, just like the loss of memory of other beings caused by mind of the demons. Just as the loss of memory, dream vision and the possession of evil spirits are caused in other beings due to mind of demons etc., the things happen due to minds of prosperous *Yogīs*; the king *Sāraṇa* had a dream by the influence of the *Ārya-Mahākātyāna*, *Vemacitra* was defeated due to the foresters' minds anguish. Similarly, due to a particular consciousness of some other being there is produced a transformation in other beings stopping the life organ as such. By death is meant cutting off stream of existence."

We have seen earlier that *Sautrāntikas* in their attempt to defend the reality of the external objects had raised the phenomenal question of death. In reply to this Vasubandhu explains the phenomena of death according to the traditions of *Vijñānavāda*. First of all, here we should admit that mind

32. Kochumuttom, op.cit., p.192.

is great force in itself and it has the greatest potentiality of causing many many things in the physique of other human beings. The mental power is even responsible for causing the death of somebody. The mental power is capable of creating many things at the phenomenal level. Keeping this in mind Vasubandhu interprets death as disruption of the individual stream of consciousness, which would keep on ever flowing. In other words, we may say that death is a particular type of transformation caused by a particular consciousness of another being. In order to prove that mental force is very effective Vasubandhu quotes some cases from the scriptures. In all the cases we find that sages' or the demons' mental force is always the cause and its effect is outwardly produced either in good or bad actions. This can be illustrated differently. The use of magical powers by the sages either for the welfare or destruction of others may be cited as an example. In all such cases the cause is present in the minds of sages or the demons but the effect is produced in the form of actions outside. This is sufficient to prove that the mental power is capable of even causing a death. It is well known that it was possible for the knowers of the charms to wipe off the venom from a man smitten by a serpent. They could perform this action just by their mental disposition only. It may be noted that Vasubandhu has cited such cases in order to prove that the mental force is responsible for effecting changes in others. This only shows that consciousness is real and all outwardly manifestations are just mere representations of the consciousness. Kochumuttom observes, "Again Vasubandhu seems to believe that the phenomenal world is an interplay of such minds, and that representations issuing from one mind can act on those issuing from other minds, the real nature of the individuals still remaining unaffected...... Thus Vasubandhu maintains that death as well as the fact that it can be caused by others, is real experience of the phenomenal level of existence, namely saṃsāra...... It may be further noted that in the yogic tradition of India, mental power is the greatest force that can be used for the advantage or disadvantage of others. So it is quite normal for Vasubandhu to make so much of it".[33] As far as the Buddhist tradition is concerned, death is not something permanent but it is only cutting off life process for a certain while. Accordingly an individual stream

---

33. Kochumuttom, op.cit., pp.192-193.

of consciousness is ever flowing. Its stream is really never cut off in between. In order to prove this Vasubandhu uses a word *'sabhāgasantativiccheda'* -meaning thereby that this stream of consciousness (which is always uninterrupted in a continuous flow) is cut off temporarily. He has treated death as a special type of transformation, which is to be regarded as anti-living organism.(*jīvitendriyavirodhinī*).

In other words we may say that according to the Buddhist traditions death is only a special type of transformation of ever going life process. This transformation apparently looks like a death in the empirical sense of the term, but in reality this is only a change in the life process. It must be observed that the transformation may be caused by the mental power of somebody in the physique of another person.

कथं वा दण्डकारण्यशून्यत्वमृषिकोपतः ।

यदि परविज्ञप्तिविशेषाधिपत्यात् सत्वानां मरणं नेष्यते, मनोदण्डस्य हि महासावद्यत्वं साधयता भगवतोपालिर्गृहपतिः पृष्ठः - कच्चित्ते गृहपते ! श्रूतम् केन तानि दण्डकारण्यानि मातङ्गारण्यानि कलिङ्गारण्यानि शून्यानि मेध्यीभूतानि ? तेनोक्तम् - श्रुतं मे भो गोतम ! ऋषीणां मनःप्रदोषेणेति ।

"How was it that the *Daṇḍaka* forest was reduced to nothingness by the anger of the sages ? If the death of other beings is not acceptable (to you) due to the particular consciousness of others; (how is it) that the *Upāli* householder was asked by the Lord proving that the mental torture is a great punishment. "O householder, have you heard that the *Daṇḍaka* forest, *Mātaṅga*-forest and *Kaliṅga*-forest were emptied and made suitable for sacrifices? It was said by him, "Oh, Gautama, I have heard that it was (caused) due to mental rage of the sages".

We have seen above that the mental power is a great force capable of affecting the others' mind. The anguish or the mental rage is also capable of affecting others minds. The *Vijñānavādins* realising that the *Sautrāntikas* might still not be satisfied with these arguments are trying to remove thier doubts as far as the mental force is concerned. They (*Vijñānavādins*) are asking the opponents, if due to a particular consciousness others' death is not acceptable to them, then how are you going to explain the *Sūtra* of the Lord (the Lord asked the householder *Upāli*, "O householder, have you heard that the *Daṇḍaka*-forest, *Mātaṅga* forest and *Kaliṅga* forest were emptied and made suitable for sacrifices?" The householder replied, 'O Gautama, I have heard that it was (caused) due to the mental rages of the sages". It must be noted that these various forests were cleared off the wild beats by the mental rages of the sages and not any human element was involved therein. This was achieved by the mental force of the sages and this mental force in itself is the consciousness. *Daṇḍaka*-forest, *Mātaṅga*-forest and *Kaliṅga*-forest were forests where there was huge habitations before the Lord Buddha. *'Śūnya'* means that they were made empty and *'medhyībhūtānī'* means that human beings and wild beats were removed from there and they were made suitable for the sacrifices because of being devoid of urine etc. It must be understood that the instance quoted in this connection only shows that actions were caused due to the mental power of the sages, which again proves that only the consciousness is real.

मनोदण्डो महावद्यः कथं वा तेन सिध्यति ।। २० ।।

यद्येवं कल्पते, तदभिप्रसन्नैरमानुषैस्तद्वासिनः सत्वा उत्सादिताः, न त्वृषीणां मनः प्रदोषान्मृता इत्येवं कथं तेन कर्मणा मनोदण्डः कायवाग्दण्डाभ्यां महावद्यतमः सिद्धो भवति? तन्मनःप्रदोषमात्रेण तावतां सत्वानां मरणात् सिध्यति ।

"Mental torture is a great punishment, how it is proved by that ? If it is imagined that those human beings living in these forests were killed by the super human beings, who were pleased by the sages, and that these creatures were not killed by the sages mental anguish, then this being so, then how is it proved that the mental torture is a greater punishment than the body and the oral torture? (On the other hand) it becomes proved that this is possible, the death of so many beings was caused by the mental rage (of the sages)".

Vasubandhu is here citing all these scriptural evidences to prove that the mental power is something really very effective on the phenomenal level. A basic question is asked: how these forests were empited and made suitable for sacrificial rites ? Were those super human beings really happy with those sages, for whom these inhabitants were destroyed and thus the forests were made empty? There is also a second question involved in process which is really important for our contextual discussion. Was this act of emptying the forests carried out by the bodily and oral punishment (by those super human beings)? Then the answer is in the negative. Our text says that this act of emptying the forests and making these forests really suitable for the sacrificial rites was carried out by the mental rage or anguish. This indirectly proves that this punishment is more torturous that the bodily and oral torture. Another important point involved in this process is very useful for our purpose because this only exhibits that mental force i.e., the mental anguish (again at the consciousness level only) is responsible for the outer actions. Thus the whole process simply shows that the mental force is very effective in carrying out the external actions. The basic idea behind quoting the scriptual evidences is to narrate an instance in which the sages were able to carry out external actions, which only proves that the consciousness is the true reality and all the external objects and actions are mere manifestations of this consciousness. We have already seen above that how even the phenomena of death has been interpreted in the light of *Vijñānavāda* saying that death is a transformational change or the disruption of the individual stream of consciousness.[34]

यदि विज्ञप्तिमात्रमेवेदम् , परचित्तविदः किं परचित्तं जानन्ति, अथ न ? किञ्चातः ?

यदि न जानन्ति, कथं परचित्तविदो भवन्ति अथ जानन्ति, परचित्तविदां ज्ञानमययाथं कथम् ?

"If everything is consciousness, do the knowers of others mind (really) know others mind or not? How does it matter? If they do not know, how are they knowers of others mind? If they know, then how the knowledge of the knowers of others mind is real?"

Uptil now we have been observing that Vasubandhu has been very successfully meeting all the objections of his opponents, the *Sautrāntikas*. Even now they (the opponents) are not satisfied with the answer suggested by the *Vijñānavādins*. They are raising altogether a different point with regard to the reality of the knowledge gained by those, who claim to be the knowers of others mind. The point is: whether the knowledge is real or not. As a matter of fact, to

---

34. Cf. Vasubandhu gives three statements in the regard:
(i) मरणं परविज्ञप्तिविशेषाद् विक्रिया यथा ।
(ii) परविज्ञप्तिविशेषाधिपत्यात् परेषां जीवितेन्द्रियविरोधिनी काचित् विक्रियोत्पद्यते।
(iii) सभागसन्ततिविच्छेदाख्यं मरणं भवतीति वेदितव्यम् ।।

the *Vijñānavādins* this hardly matters. But the oppents are still sticking to the position of holding the external objects to be real. Who is really the knower of others mind? Then this presumed that a *Yogī,* who has attained the stage of *paracittavidabhijñā,* is really the knower of others mind. *Abhijñā* is a special type of power which is acquired after deep meditation. *Abhijñās* (particular type of power gained out of meditation) are five in number: (i) *Ṛdhividha,* (ii) *Divyaśtrotra,* (iii) *Divyacakṣu,* (iv) *Paracittajñāna* and (v) *Pūrvanidāsānusmṛti. Paracittavidabhijñā* is a special power of knowledge by which one can acquire the knowledge of others mind. The point is: if one cannot really know others mind, how can he be called a *paracittavid*? The opponents i.e., *Sautrāntikas* are asking the *Vijñānavādins* about those, who claim to know the mind of others. They maintain that in such a situation the grasper and the graspable distinction remains there because at that moment the *paracittavid* would be *grāhya* (graspable) and the *abhijñā* would be the *grāhaka* (grasper). These two i.e., *grāhya* and the *grāhaka* would be separately visible to the *yogī*. In such a situation the *yogī* cannot claim to be the knower of reality because he is distinctly perceiving the *grāhya* and *grāhaka*. In other words we may say that the subject-object distinction would still remain. As long as the distinction between subject and the object remains, such a knowledge cannot be said to be true reality. When the true real knowledge is obtained, the distinction between the subject and the object is removed and the *yogī* rises above the distinction of dualism of *grāhaya* and *grāhaka*.

यथा

स्वचित्तज्ञानम्

तदपि कथमयथार्थम् ?

अज्ञानाद् यथा बुद्धस्य गोचरः ।। २१ ।।

यथा तन्निरभिलाप्येनात्मना बुद्धानां गोचरः, तथा तदज्ञानात् तदुभयं न यथार्थम्, वितथप्रतिभासतया गाह्य-ग्राहकविकल्पस्याप्रहीणत्वात् ।

"Just as one's own knowledge of one's mind is unreal. How is it that the knowledge of one's mind is unreal? Because in that way in which the mind is known to the enlightened ones, it is unknown to the ordinary man. Just as mind is known to the enlightened in its ineffable nature, similarly by its not knowing (both one's own mind and others mind), such a knowledge is unreal because of false distinction between graspable and grasper is not (yet) given up and there is still the presence of subject-object distinction."

At this juncture the text i.e., *Viṃśatikā* comes to an end. It has been previously explained that those, who claim to be the knowers of others mind, really do not know others mind. Similarly one's own knowledge of one's own mind is also unreal. It has been shown above that probably only the *yogī* can know others mind due to his special power of meditation. But it is concluded here that the *yogī* also really does not know others mind. Just as all the human beings really do not know their past *citta* (mind) and future *citta* (mind), similarly the special power of the *yogī* known as *paracittābhijñā* really does not know others' mind. On account of the meditation the *yogī* can reflect others mind as his own. And in the same manner he reflects the past and the future events. In reality he understands the *ghāhya* (graspable) portion of his own *citta* (mind) as *paracitta* (others mind) and that is why he is designated as *paracittavīd* (knower of others mind). Whereas, on the contrary, the fact is that the Lord Buddha really knows the ineffable nature of one's own mind and also of others mind. But an ordinary human being really does not know even his own mind. Similarly the *yogī* really does not know others mind. In one's own mind's knowledge of a human being and in the others mind's knoweldge of a *yogī* there is always the presence of *grāhya* (graspable) and *grāhaka* (grasper). Both the human being and the *yogī* are never able to give up their habit of discriminating between graspable and the grasper. Moreover, there is always a false appearance of subject and object distinction in them. To quote Kochumuttom. "In these few lines Vasubandhu seems to have summarised the whole system of his thought: that every being has an ineffable and a phenomenal aspect of existence; that there are a multiplicity of enlightened beings, who alone can know things in their ineffable aspect of existence; that the saṃsāric existence is characterised by the idiosyncrasy for subject-object distinction, due to which one in the state of *saṃsāra* can perceive only the unreal form (*vitatha-pratibhāsa*) of one's own consciousness."[35]

---

35. Kochumuttom, op.cit. p.195.

अनन्तविनिश्चयप्रभेदागाधागाम्भीर्यायां विज्ञप्तिमात्रतायाम्,
विज्ञप्तिमात्रतासिद्धिः स्वशक्तिसदृशी मया ।
कृतेयं सर्वथा सा तु न चिन्त्या ।।

सर्वप्रकारा तु सा मादृशैश्चिन्तयितुं न शक्यते, तर्काविषय-त्वात् । कस्य पुनः सा सर्वथा गोचरः ? इत्याह –

बुद्धगोचरः ।। २२ ।।

बुद्धानां हि सा भगवतां सर्वप्रकारं गोचरः सर्वाकार-सर्वज्ञेयज्ञानाविघाताद् ।

इति विंशतिका विज्ञप्तिमात्रतासिद्धिः ।।

कृतिरियमाचार्यवसुबन्धोः ।।

"The theory of consciousness being of innumerable possibilities of various divisions and immensely deep; this ..k of theory of consciousness only has been composed by me according to my own ability. It is not possible to discuss all its aspects. This theory of consciousness only cannot be discussed by me in all its aspects because it is beyond the limit of logic. To whom it is known in all its aspects? (Then) it is said, it is known (in all its aspects) to the enlightened Lords because only their knowledge is unobstructed and in all sorts of knowable things.

Here ends the work known as *Vijñaptimātratāsiddih* written by the preceptor Vasubandhu."

Vasubandhu concludes the text *Viṃśatikā* observing that this theory of representation of consciousness only is capable of admitting innumerable possibilities, various divisions and the whole system in itself is very deep and subtle. In all his humility he frankly admits that this work has been written by him according to his best of ability. Moreover, it is simply not possible for him to discuss and comprehend all its various aspects, shades, meanings and interpretations because the whole system of consciousness can never be studied with the help of logic. Then naturally the question arises: who is realy capable of comprehending this in all its aspects. Then the author Vasubandhu offers his answer that this is simply to be properly comprehended by the enlightened ones only because it is only their knowledge, which is really unobstructed in all sorts of knowable objects or things.

Appendix No.1

त्रिंशिकाविज्ञप्तिकारिकाः

आत्मधर्मोपचारो हि विविधो यः प्रवर्तते ।
विज्ञानपरिणामेऽसौ परिणामः स च त्रिधा ।। १ ।।
विपाको मननाख्यश्च विज्ञप्तिर्विषयस्य च ।
तत्रालयाख्यं विज्ञानं विपाकः सर्वबीजकम् ।। २ ।।
असंविदितकोपादिस्थानविज्ञप्तिकं च तत् ।
सदा स्पर्शमनस्कारवित्संज्ञाचेतनान्वितम् ।। ३ ।।
उपेक्षा वेदना तत्रानिवृताव्याकृतं च तत् ।
तथा स्पर्शादयस्तच्च वर्तते स्रोतसौघवत् ।। ४ ।।
तस्य व्यावृत्तिरर्हत्त्वे तदाश्रित्य प्रवर्तते ।
तदालम्बं मनोनाम विज्ञानं मननात्मकम् ।। ५ ।।
क्लेशैश्चतुर्भिः सहितं निवृताव्याकृतैः सदा ।
आत्मदृष्ट्यात्ममोहात्ममानात्मस्नेहसंज्ञितैः ।। ६ ।।
यत्रजस्तन्मयैरन्यैः स्पर्शाद्यैश्चार्हतो न तत् ।
न निरोधसमापत्तौ मार्गे लोकोत्तरे न च ।। ७ ।।
द्वितीयः परिणामोऽयं तृतीयः षड्विधस्य या ।
विषयस्योपलब्धिः सा कुशलाकुशलाद्वया ।। ८ ।।
सर्वत्रगैर्विनियतैः कुशलैश्चैतसैरसौ ।
सम्प्रयुक्ता तथा क्लेशैरुपक्लेशैस्त्रिवेदना ।। ९ ।।
आद्याः स्पर्शादयश्छन्दाधिमोक्षस्मृतयः सह ।
समाधिधीभ्यां नियताः श्रद्धाथ ह्रीरपत्रपा ।। १० ।।

अलोभादित्रयं वीर्यं प्रश्रब्धिः साप्रमादिका ।
अहिंसा कुशलाः क्लेशा रागप्रतिघमूढयः ।। ११ ।।
मानदृग्विचिकित्साश्च क्रोधोपनहने पुनः ।
म्रक्षः प्रदाश ईर्ष्याथ मात्सर्यं सह मायया ।। १२ ।।
शाठ्यं मदो विहिंसा ह्रीरत्रपा स्त्यानमुद्धवः ।
आश्रद्धयमथ कौसीद्यं प्रमादो मुषिता स्मृतिः ।। १३ ।।
विक्षेपोऽसम्प्रजन्यं च कौकृत्यं मिद्धमेव च ।
वितर्कश्च विचारश्चेत्युपक्लेशा द्वये द्विधा ।। १४ ।।
पञ्चानां मूलविज्ञाने यथाप्रत्ययमुद्भवः ।
विज्ञानानां सह न वा तरङ्गाणां यथा जले ।। १५ ।।
मनोविज्ञानसम्भूतिः सर्वदासंज्ञिकादृते ।
समापत्तिद्वयान्मिद्धान्मूर्च्छनादप्यचित्तकात् ।। १६ ।।
विज्ञानपरिणामोऽयं विकल्पो यद् विकल्प्यते ।
तेन तन्नास्ति तेनेदं सर्वं विज्ञप्तिमात्रकम् ।। १७ ।।
सर्वबीजं हि विज्ञानं परिणामस्तथा तथा ।
यात्यन्योऽन्यवशाद् येन विकल्पः स स जायते ।। १८ ।।
कर्मणो वासना ग्राहद्वयवासनया सह ।
क्षीणे पूर्वविपाकेऽन्यद् विपाकं जनयन्ति सह ।। १९ ।।
येन येन विकल्पेन यद् यद् वस्तु विकल्प्यते ।
परिकल्पित एवासौ स्वभावो न स विद्यते ।। २० ।।
परतन्त्रस्वभावस्तु विकल्पः प्रत्ययोद्भवः ।
निष्पन्नस्तस्य पूर्वेण सदा रहितता तु या ।। २१ ।।
अत एव स नैवान्यो नानन्यः परतन्त्रतः ।
अनित्यतादिवद् वाच्यो नादृष्टेऽस्मिन् स दृष्यते ।। २२ ।।
त्रिविधस्य स्वभावस्य त्रिविधां निःस्वाभावताम् ।
सन्धाय सर्वधर्माणां देशिता निःस्वभावता ।। २३ ।।

प्रथमो लक्षणेनैव निःस्वभावोऽपरः पुनः ।
न स्वयम्भाव एतस्येत्यपरा निःस्वभावता ।। २४ ।।
धर्माणां परमार्थश्च स यतस्तथताऽपि सः।
सर्वकालं तथाभावात् सैव विज्ञप्तिमात्रता ।। २५ ।।
यावद् विज्ञप्तिमात्रत्वे विज्ञानं नावतिष्ठति ।
ग्राहद्वयस्यानुशयस्तावन्न विनिवर्तते ।। २६ ।।
विज्ञप्तिमात्रमेवेदमित्यपि ह्युपलम्भतः ।
स्थापयन्नग्रतः किञ्चित् तन्मात्रे नावतिष्ठते ।। २७ ।।
यदा त्वालम्बनं ज्ञानं नैवोपलभते तदा ।
स्थितं विज्ञानमात्रत्वे ग्राह्याभावे तदग्रहात् ।। २८ ।।
अचित्तोऽनुपलम्भोऽसौ ज्ञानं लोकोत्तरं च तत् ।
आश्रयस्य परावृत्तिर्द्विधा दौष्ठुल्यहानितः ।। २९ ।।
स एवानास्रवो धातुरचिन्त्यः कुशलो ध्रुवः ।
सुखो विमुक्तिकायोऽसौ धर्माख्योऽयं महामुने ।। ३० ।।